Asset-Based Community Development: Looking Back To Look Forward

In conversation with John McKnight about the
heritage of ABCD and its place in the world today

Cormac Russell

"There are many lines in this short, insightful book that resonated with me. We are indeed too often 'looking for solutions in well-lit places, instead of revealing the invisible all around us.' Cormac's book, and the voice of John McKnight and others contained within, does shine a light on the invisible. It makes us question what we thought we knew about people's capacity and agency and then it calls on us to change our behaviours accordingly.

As with many radical concepts, the prevailing culture works against change. Too often, in practice I have seen ABCD reduced to producing an asset map as part of a consultation on a community plan. The system has a strong pull towards acting in its own self-interest. It was a pleasure, therefore, to spend time with this book and be reminded of the radical origins of the concept and to think again about what might be possible if we thought differently about ourselves, our communities and our governance."

Jennifer Wallace
Head of Policy
Carnegie UK Trust (United Kingdom & Rep. of Ireland)

"This book is a gift. A gift for those who love John McKnight and Asset-Based Community Development and a gift from Cormac Russell who has captured the story of John's life and the people who have influenced John with such eloquence. This book is a pleasure to read as the interview style helps us feel like we are reading a live story, a 'fireside chat with John,' while giving us important, quotable insights into John's thinking. Cormac is one of the few people who could write this book. He understands ABCD almost as well as John and can therefore help the reader to engage in the fine nuances of John's brilliance. I highly recommend this book for change makers around the world."

Paul Born
Tamarack Institute

Co-CEO Tamarack & Director, Vibrant Communities
Author of several books including: "Deepening Community. Finding Joy
Together in Chaotic times." (Canada)

"Through insightful and thought-provoking interviews with John, Cormac has certainly given ABCD animators and connectors around the world a deep understanding and appreciation of the rich heritage and history of ABCD. He has provided the trumpet call for all to continually understand the past and faithfully journey into the future of being within communities.

As a public servant, Cormac has provided me with practical handles and clear perspectives, giving impetus for courage and boldness to arise in order to go beyond the comfort zone and safe facade of institutions.

Through the endearing and exceedingly deep conversations with John, I seem to have encountered him face-to-face, and heard the soulful voice of a man with a keen mind, a big heart and a deep belief in the power of communities. This book certainly honors a man whose lifetime work has proliferated to different communities in many countries.

I heartily recommend Looking Back to Look Forward to all who believe that our communities indeed have all the assets to pursue and exceed our own dreams and aspirations."

Mr. Phua Chun Yat
Head of Planning and Organisation Development
AMKFSC Community Services Ltd, (Singapore)

"I highly recommend Looking Back to Look Forward to anyone with a passion to unleash the power of communities for positive social change. Over the past five years, Wellspring Foundation has worked closely with Cormac Russell and Nurture Development to help 49 schools connected to 484 villages in Rwanda make a significant shift from scarcity to abundance through Asset-Based Community Development (ABCD). The results have been astonishing. As communities step up and take ownership over the education of their own children they are accomplishing things that aid agencies and governments typically spend years trying to accomplish: drop outs are reducing, children are receiving nutritious meals, school infrastructure is being improved, and teachers are being better supported, all through community effort. By some estimates, community investment is outpacing government investment 3:1. In most cases, Rwandan communities have realized that ABCD is merely re-introducing them to a language they already had before the 'culture killers' came. I have never had the privilege of meeting John McKnight and so I found it fascinating to gain an insider's view of his extraordinary life, his influences, and how ABCD was birthed. So stoke a fire, grab a cup of hot tea, and join the conversation."

Richard Taylor
Co-Founder and Rwanda Country Director
The Wellspring Foundation for Education (Rwanda)

"This is a timely and important book, taking us on a wondrous journey through the evolution of John McKnight's life and work. In it we meet people John considers most influential for him. In the process, it also grounds us in the work and ideas of people who have informed and shaped what has come to be known as Asset-Based Community Development (ABCD).

As John's own thinking has moved from a critical analysis of institutions and professionals to a practical approach for citizens and their associations, and then gradually into a varied and adaptive set of different approaches that seek to fit the local context and asset base, ABCD has become a kind of worldwide movement. Here we learn through guided conversations between Cormac and John how each of these one-of-a-kind people informed his thought. As importantly – it also features Cormac's own take on things as he looks forward to how ABCD principles and practices can be applied to an ever-widening circle of people and places.

Riveting as a public speaker and storyteller, one of John's gifts is that he has constantly sought to deepen his own understanding of 'how things work,' as these intellectual and personal friends so aptly demonstrate. Throughout, his core values have been consistent, but his ability to deepen and reweave his analysis based on new experiences and learning from others is truly remarkable. And his capacity to deliver his evolving analysis to a wide range of audience, through stories and clear summary principles, is – for most of us who have travelled with him - unrivalled.

In terms of the people John describes here, it is noteworthy that these folks are all renegades, and most had a following of their own. They are independent, radical (going to the 'root of things'), and feisty. John tried to understand them in their own terms and his descriptions of their role in his own thinking are telling. His measure of their role and value for us all was this: 'how does this person help me understand my experience?'

And what a cast of characters it is! Ivan Illich and 'counter-productivity,' Bob Mendelsohn and the 'medicalization of everyday life,' Saul Alinksy and the 'basics of organizing for power,' Judith Snow on 'welcoming the stranger,' Jerry Miller and the illusion of believing anything gets better by institutionalizing "dangerous" people, Bob Rodale and faithful stewardship of the land and its bounty; Frank Haiman on the value of every person – especially those at the edges, Peter Block and how to recognize and enhance the "abundant community," Stan Hallett and the necessity of citizen associations and alternatives to the kind of modern technology that breaks down rather than enhances community, and Jody Kretzmann, who as co-founder of the ABCD, has been the personal embodiment of ABCD values in practice.

In exploring these various people, Cormac puts his finger on the rich veins of energy and insight that run through John's thought. When Cormac notes, for example, that honoring the heritage of ABCD will require that we all resist the deeply embedded tendency to 'fix, save and deliver,' he is astutely summarizing the core of ABCD as an alternative to top-down and outside-in 'help' that is so typically offered by professional service delivery systems, and that curtail or erode the prospects for citizen action and the rejuvenation of varied forms of local community life.

But what is perhaps most remarkable about this book and set of conversations, is that Cormac not only goes deeply into these friendships, he also goes beyond them. He adds his own take, and it is an extraordinarily important take. He is at his best when he looks forward, and wonders 'out loud' about where it is all going. His capacity to turn a phrase may actually rival John, such as, 'we are not self-reliant but other reliant..' or, 'the importance of moving from what's wrong to what's strong.'

Just as we can be glad that Cormac helps John put these people and their influence into perspective, we can be glad that we have Cormac and his own growing network of people and learning sites. John is still searching, no doubt, and thankfully, so is Cormac. Cormac's own clarity about the key principles of ABCD and his creative and tenacious way of applying them in varied settings through his impressive work with Nurture Development, in the UK and across the globe, auger well for the future of the movement."

Tom Dewar -Senior Faculty member of the ABCD Institute. Formerly Co-Director of the Aspen Institute's Roundtable on Community Change and taught at Johns Hopkins' School for Advanced International Studies, helping direct its Center for Democratic Development

"What's most stirred in me after reading this book twice is an overwhelming sense of comfort, settling into my bones and heart from several directions.

The comfort of mentorship. From its oldest roots, hospitality asks both the host and the stranger to answer three questions: Where have you been? Why are you here? And where are you going? John, simply and with an open heart, answered those three questions for himself in the pages of this book, and has offered a gentle and open invitation to each of us on the doorstep of this book to do the same, that we might plant the seeds of hospitality around us through sharing our stories.

The comfort of legacy. Genuine legacy is not what you are remembered for by others, but rather how the world is different because you were in it. John's firm insistence on bringing the theory of ABCD into real community change, and his ability to tell countless stories about change, is a legacy worth learning from and living into.

The comfort of homecoming. Reading this book caused me to return, over and over again, to a deep knowing in me that what John is saying about community—and 'its counterfeits'— is true. It offers hope to me that if I follow this community-building path it will take me home to what I know is true in my bones: Everyone has gifts and everyone has place in community.

The comfort of libation. This book is a libation, a pouring of wisdom into the collective bowl of community life. John's humble and clear gratitude for those who have mentored him asks each of us to give up the idea of the self-made person and insist on the community-building wisdom that we exist only because of the ones who have come before us. And to heed the underlying message that this makes us obligated to be clear about who we are, since others are depending on us now and in the future.

Thank you, John and Cormac, for a book that is simple to understand, and has a depth worth a lifetime of pursuit."

Bruce Anderson, ABCD Institute Faculty, Co-Founder of Community Activators, Neighborhood and Community Development, Involving Institutions (Vashon, WA)

"This book is inspirational reading for anyone involved in community action, organizing and development. Cormac Russell's interviews with John McKnight do not only illustrate the underlying principles of Asset-Based Community Development. ABCD is placed in a social and philosophical context throughout the interviews. As in Cormac's teaching of ABCD, there is several layers of knowledge in the stories that is shared by the two of them in the interviews.

Cormac makes John McKnight's work and inspiriting friendships unfold in unison, while philosophy and social theory is intertwined. John McKnight talks about friends that influenced him, like the academic thinker Ivan Illich and community activist Judith Snow. He shows how their lived experiences and theories on topics like clientization and medicalization inspired ways to make changes by focusing on assets in community development.

John McKnight's life experiences, influenced by critical thinkers and activists, forms a backdrop for his reflections on phenomena like co-production and how the role of helping professions may undermine the autonomy of citizens. John McKnight's voice comes across as uplifting, as he advocates a change in perspective to identify individual and collective resources. This is not presented as a 'mindset,' as in the trendy positive psychology, but as awareness of individual gifts and community resources, which also implies a strengthening of associational life and local democracy.

The reflections about what constitutes a society and how community members may change it, is not only food for thought, but also inspiration to act. The interviews show how Asset-Based Community

Development was born from critical thinking, humbleness, and respect for citizens and local cultures, to empower local communities and make changes that matters both locally and globally.

As in the Asset focus of ABCD, the book is genuinely positive and resource focused, looking back to look forward."

Prof. Rita Agdal,
Head of the community work section, Western Norway University of Applied Sciences (Norway)

"In Looking back to look forward, Cormac Russell conveys a rich narrative history of community development in its various forms, via the major figures in the field. It is an ideal introduction to Asset-Based Community Development (ABCD) and as an explanation of its historical influences for those who are already familiar with ABCD.

For me, the book was profoundly inspiring, prompting me to catch up with literature from John McKnight, Peter Block, and Ivan Illich. I came to realise that within local communities are 'community assets': individuals, their associations, their institutions, the land they occupy, and their means of exchange and interaction. Critical among these are the gifts, skills and passions of community members, who can produce much of what the community needs to live well and to prosper. I came to understand more clearly how community-facing institutions and professions tend to ignore these and other 'community assets,' and treat communities as though they were deficient, creating more dependence on professions and institutions to fulfil community functions. Contrary to the typical professional approach, the ABCD approach seeks to unveil the possibilities within communities to create full and satisfying lives for all of its members, creating opportunities and overcoming or accommodating fallibilities. ABCD provides a description of how communities can thrive.

Looking Back to Look Forward has relevance both to place-based local communities, and organisations and professions that interact with these communities. While the book applies primarily to local communities, I found that many of the insights apply to other groups outside and inside of organisations (professions, clubs, associations, online groups, etc), who may see themselves in a 'community-like' way. I strongly enjoyed this book and recommend it to anyone who believes that ordinary people can do extraordinary things when they discover, connect and mobilise what they have to offer."

Dr Steven Shorrock
Chartered Psychologist and Chartered Ergonomist
and Human Factors Specialist
Adjunct Associate Professor, University of The Sunshine Coast,
Australia

This book is dedicated with love to my wife Colleen, who is rooted enough in everyday life to keep me grounded and present to the things that really matter.

Acknowledgements

As with every such enterprise, the writing of this short book has been a community endeavour. I owe John McKnight special thanks for his generosity of spirit. His willingness to extend his time and energy to ensure we captured the historical and conceptual details correctly was centrally important to the final text.

Sincere thanks to all those who reviewed the many drafts of the book including Paul Born, Jim Diers, Tom Dewar, Al Etmanski, Martin Simon and Judith Snow. My particular thanks to Judith Snow for her mentoring and support, and for agreeing to allow me to use her painting *Altered State* on the front cover of the first edition of this book.

Photo: Georg Lulich 2014

ABOUT THE AUTHOR

CORMAC RUSSELL is an internationally recognised thought leader, trainer and speaker in Asset-Based Community Development (ABCD). He has published extensively in professional journals on Asset-Based Community Development approaches to Probation, Ageing Well, Community Housing, Community Development in the Global South and Inclusion.

Cormac is the Managing Director of Nurture Development, an ABCD training, research and consultancy organisation that has worked worldwide with governments, NGOs, and communities since 1996. He is also a faculty member of the ABCD Institute, Northwestern University, Illinois, and Director of ABCD Europe.

Cormac —a long-time friend and collaborator with Professor John McKnight — is passionate about curating the "backstory" of Asset-Based Community Development and the next chapter of the approach. This is the first in a series of books he is authoring on the subject.

Cormac is father to five boys and is married to Colleen. They live in South County Dublin, Ireland. Over the course of the last 20 years, Cormac has supported the establishment of more than 30 ABCD learning sites in Rwanda, South Sudan, Kenya, Canada, Sweden, Ireland and the UK. He is driven by a passionate belief in the importance of localism, economic and environmental sovereignty, and is a strong advocate for the protection of indigenous living and social justice.

Table of Contents

Appendices

Foreword: A River Runs Through John by Al Etmanski

There is a warm line between you, your heroes and their mentors that unites memory and imagination. I witnessed this in 1995 at the first gathering of the Asset-Based Community Development Institute. John McKnight opened the gathering providing an overview of ABCD bedrock—asset-focused, internally reliant and relationship-driven.

Then he paused, looked each one of us in the eye and said. "That's what I've learned. I give these concepts to you. I trust you to take them to the next step."

Aside from a few polite comments, 20 of us left the room in silence. Perhaps we were tired. It was late and many of us had travelled long distances. In fact, we were stunned. We woke the next morning and realized we had been blessed. John, the man we dearly admired, had just handed everything over to us. The division between him and us had dissolved.

In retrospect, this was classic John—open-hearted and generous. When he was offered money to create an institutional centre for his ABCD work he declined. Instead, he and his co-founder Jody Kretzmann invited a number of community organizers from across North America to join them.

Asset-Based Community Development has never gone out of style and it has never been more relevant. Indeed, it is the only way it has ever been done. Today, it curates an international movement that nurtures the capacity of citizens, families, neighbourhoods and communities to resolve their challenges.

That is why Cormac Russell's new book, *Looking Back to Look Forward*, is such a gift. As one of the newest members of the ABCD network, he immersed himself in its roots by visiting John at his Chicago home. Cormac is from Ireland, which must have fired up John's Celtic roots. I imagine their conversation flowing over concepts as pure as time and as fresh as tomorrow. How I wish I had been a drop of water in their whisky glasses.

Thanks to Cormac's pilgrimage, our conceptual ancestry has risen to the surface in this highly readable and essential book. Some of them we know —some we should. Jody Kretzmann, Judith Snow, Saul Alinsky, Ivan Illich, Robert Rodale, Frank Haiman, Robert Mendelsohn, Jerome Miller, Stanley Hallet and Peter Block. Their wisdom is ennobling. Linking our humble efforts to theirs and yours.

Looking Back to Look Forward is the river running through John McKnight. It reminds us that when we are in flow, our activities and those of others, past and future merge into one. The world is made fresh and we are no longer as alone as we thought.

Now it really is up to us.

Section One: Setting the Scene

1.1 Prelude

This is the third edition of *Asset-Based Community Development (ABCD): Looking Back to Look Forward.* The first edition was published to coincide with a celebration of the last 20 years of the ABCD Institute, and the associated ABCD Festival in England (June 15 – 19, 2015).

While the Asset-Based Community Development story includes hundreds, if not thousands, of people, I have started my inquiry with John McKnight. Ultimately over the next few years, during my ongoing inquiry into the evolving journey of ABCD, I will speak to many, many others. I have known John McKnight for nearly 20 years; he is a bona fide radical and disruptive innovator, from whom I have learned most about the irreplaceable functions of communities, families and citizens.

In September 2013, I spent five days with him, learning more about his extraordinary life as a community builder, storyteller and mentor. The journey from Dublin, Ireland to get to John and his wife Marsha in Evanston, Illinois was an adventurous one, not least because my wife Colleen and I brought our three young children, Eli and Saul (our twin boys of 16 months at the time) and Isaac who was three-and-a-half years old. A transatlantic flight with three children less than four years old is enough to test even the most patient of souls. Still, both Colleen and I were so glad we had brought the boys.

John and Marsha have become such an important part of all our lives. They are first and foremost our friends—so much so that we christened one of the boys Eli "John" for John—and so having the opportunity to spend extended time together was a joy in itself.

Along with wonderful hospitality and friendship, John shared anecdotes and incisive reflections on the people who have most influenced his thinking over the last 60 years or more. We also delved deeply into his current thinking on ABCD—the approach he co-developed with Jody Kretzmann—and talked in great detail about community and society. The pages that follow contain many of those stories.

His words affirm how ABCD, as well as emerging from an intimate appreciation of what communities do naturally to grow strong and prosper, often in the face of great challenges, has been deeply embroidered with insights from some of the world's most radical thinkers, including Saul Alinsky and Ivan Illich.

I am delighted to present here an edited transcript of these interviews to illuminate the detail, the craftsmanship, the power and the elegance of ABCD—an approach which is capacity oriented—to restoring a culture of community to us all, by us all.

Saul Alinsky's seminal book, *Reveille for Radicals*, made a significant impression on John as a young man. The word "Reveille" is an appropriate choice for the title of a book that focuses on building broad-based powerful organisations. Reveille is derived from the French word réveiller, *to wake*, and is associated with a bugle, or trumpet call, used to wake military personnel at sunrise.

Asset-Based Community Development: Looking Back to Look Forward is intended to be a rousing and inspiring book that sounds a very different sort of wake-up call than *Reveille for Radicals*.

While I have no doubt that the ideas expressed in *Looking Back to Look Forward* might also act as a rallying cry for many people, they are not intended to be a call to action against an external force that is believed to hold all the power, nor an attempt to press people into service as foot soldiers for a higher cause or against a common foe.

Rather, these pages chart a radical path towards inside-out development, where local people come together to use the resources, capacities and collective power within and around them to secure freedom of expression and association for everyone. Not as foot soldiers, but as powerful, aware, interdependent citizens at the centre of a deepening democracy.

While at times outside forces need to be confronted, as in the civil rights movement, ABCD is the method designed to also mobilise the inside forces that are the basic source of community power—a power that not alone includes everyone in a process of place-based transformation but also forms the basis of holding technocracy, and corporate interests at bay.

Hence *Asset-Based Community Development: Looking Back to Look Forward* offers the reader a probing commentary on the devastating impacts of consumerism and the disabling effects of professionalisation, on citizenship and communities. Yet, whilst it presents an unflinching critique of human services and the helping professions, it also describes a sensible and coherent path to recovery with a role for institutions should they choose to support the reseeding of associational life over institutional reform.

*****

John L. McKnight is one of the world's more gifted storytellers and public intellectuals. He was raised a travelling Ohioan, having lived in seven neighbourhoods and small towns in the 18 years before he left to attend Northwestern University in Evanston, Illinois.

At university, John honed his considerable natural talent in the art of public speaking and deepened his interest in language and semantics. In so doing, he came to understand that "words don't mean, people do." And it is through this freedom of expression, and association, that democracy is made and sustained.

This short book does not seek to tell the whole story: its objectives are far more modest. Rather, it aims to:

- Draw out the key influences – the people, concepts, experiences and conditions which served to inspire and refine

John McKnight's thinking.

• Explore the heritage of Asset-Based Community Development, from John McKnight's perspective.

• Share John McKnight's current thinking about community and society.

The following edited transcript contains deep insights into John's career and the main influences on his thinking. In all, John speaks about nine of the main individuals he feels most influenced him and his thinking about community, society and ABCD. The abridged book is intentionally short, and written in a style that endeavours to stay true to the conversational flow of the interview process, and John's voice. In all, there are 11 chapters, of which nine are included as full interviews as follows:

Interview One – Saul Alinsky

Interview Two – Ivan Illich

Interview Three – Frank Haiman

Interview Four – Robert Mendelsohn

Interview Five – Robert Rodale

Interview Six – Jerome Miller

Interview Seven – Judith Snow

Interview Eight – Jody Kretzmann and Stan Hallett

Interview Nine – Peter Block

The 10th chapter aims to capture the essence of ABCD and in particular to present a coherent summary narrative by defining what I believe to be the five core principles that underpin the approach.

The final section offers some concluding remarks, by way of celebrating John's great insight on community and society as well as celebrating John himself.

For John, there is need for all of us to return to our senses, and returning to our senses is about homecoming, a re-migration back to our neighbourhoods and away from overdependence on the marketplace and technology, so that we can do the necessary work of cultivating the community way, our way. The return journey is an opportunity to learn afresh about co-operation, enduring and sustainable production of sustaining and abundant things and the reseeding of democracy. It is thus a fitting inquiry for the current time, serving to illuminate some counter-intuitive pathways towards a more sustainable and sustaining future.

At 85 years of age, John is the epitome of a human being in love with life and enchanted by the humanity of others and the ecology of the place he calls "neighbourhood". As someone who has already returned to his senses, he is totally convincing when he speaks of the capacity of neighbourhoods to restore conviviality and for people to recover for themselves a practical and sustainable ecology, a living democracy and mutual prosperity. What he now refers to as a "culture of community".

Today, John lives in Evanston, Illinois, with his wife Marsha Barnett, close by to his son Jonathon. A finer mentor and friend there never was.

A Note to the Reader

Wisdom has a special syntax; it has a recognisable rhythm, and a particular inflection that becomes most apparent in conversation and storytelling. So pull up a comfortable chair; come join me for a conversation with a very wise man about the "good life," friendship and the community way. Welcome, friend.

1.2 A Potted (Early) History of Asset-Based Community Development

If we take it for granted that Asset-Based Community Development (ABCD), as a perspective, is timeless, because it simply describes what communities do when they come together to effectively make things better where they live, and what they use to do so, despite the challenges they face, we still owe a significant debt of gratitude to John McKnight and Jody Kretzmann (Co-Directors of the ABCD Institute) for the clarity they have brought to the articulation of this perspective and the practices that flow from it. They, along with their colleagues and ABCD enthusiasts throughout the world, have curated and analysed the stories of community relatedness that illuminate the irreplaceable and invaluable functions of communities.

This third edition is not only an opportunity to celebrate their work and that of the faculty of the ABCD Institute, but also, and indeed more importantly, to celebrate the millions of local residents who on a daily basis grow their communities from inside out, having never heard the term ABCD. Some grow their communities through time banking, others through principles and practices from within the slow food movement, yet others through community arts. The variations are endless, yet all have been at the vanguard of a citizen led movement for change; having thrown their lives into becoming the counter balance to a non-sustaining and unsustainable consumer culture.

In telling the ABCD story specifically, the chronology of events brings us to start with John L. McKnight, who is one of the world's most gifted storytellers, but he is also a public intellectual and provocateur. As noted in the book he co-authored, *Abundant Communities*, "He was raised a travelling Ohioan, having lived in seven neighbourhoods and small towns in the 18 years before he left to attend Northwestern University, in Evanston, Illinois."

At university, John honed his considerable natural talent in the art of public speaking and deepened his interest in public speaking and general semantics. In so doing, he came to understand that "words don't mean, people do." It also became clear to him that people make meaning in free association with each other, and that neighbourhoods provide an opportune place for such connectedness; since it is there that people can collectively define their challenges and agree and enact the solutions that fit their local context. And it is through this freedom of expression, and association, that democracy is co-created and sustained.

After his graduation, John joined the U.S. Navy, where he spent three years in active service during the Korean War. On returning to Chicago in the mid 1950's, he worked with the Chicago Commission for Human Relations, the first municipal civil rights agency. This is where he learned the craft of Alinsky-style community organising.

From 1960 to1963, John was Executive Director of the Illinois Division of the American Civil Liberties Union, where he organised local chapters. John was then recruited by the federal government, where he worked under the Kennedy administration in a new agency which started the Affirmative Action Program. Later, he was appointed the Midwest Director of the United States Commission on Civil Rights, where he again worked on local civil rights issues within local neighbourhood organisations.

In 1969, John returned once again to Northwestern University, this time to help establish a newly minted department, the Center for Urban Affairs. The previous year had been fraught with heartbreak and civil strife. Martin Luther King Jr. was assassinated in April, and Bobby Kennedy was shot in June of 1968. Civil protest had become the new norm. *The Kerner Report* (The National Advisory Commission on Civil Disorders, known as the Kerner Commission was established by President Lyndon B. Johnson to investigate the causes of the 1967 race riots in the United States and to provide recommendations for the future) was published that same year and the National Advisory Commission on Civil Disorders noted, "Our nation is moving toward two societies, one black, one white— separate and unequal."

It was against this tragic and disquieting backdrop that in 1968 Northwestern University opened the Center for Urban Affairs—now the Institute for Policy Research (IPR)—where a multidisciplinary team of researchers (including John McKnight, Ray Mack, Stanley Hallett, Jody Kretzmann, Andrew Gordon, Fred Du Bow, Paul Arntson, Tom Dewar, Malcolm Bush, Art Lyons, Denis Detzel, Alice Murray), committed themselves to seeking a better understanding of the "real-world causes and consequences" of urban poverty.

IPR grew out of a faculty working group on metropolitan studies led by Raymond Mack, a sociologist best known for his groundbreaking work on race. He became the new centre's first director.

The centre got off to an auspicious start thanks to a sizeable Ford Foundation grant, which allowed it to expand its interdisciplinary faculty from three to 12 researchers and to undertake a number of groundbreaking pieces of research.

This included one particular endeavour by Professor John McKnight, Professor Jody Kretzmann and 18 of their associates, which was to become a cornerstone for Asset-Based Community Development. In the late 1980s, this endeavour saw John McKnight and Jody Kretzmann travel across North America, visiting more than 300 neighbourhoods in 20 cities. Along with a core group of associates, they set out to identify the basic building blocks of healthy urban neighbourhoods.

This four-year odyssey brought them into personal contact with thousands of local people who had hitherto largely been labelled and defined by their issues—unemployment, teenage pregnancies, poor housing. When John and Jody entered these communities, they had the presence of mind to shift the focus from deficiencies and problems and to ask a different set of questions than was typical of academic "types." They wanted to understand, despite multiple socio-economic and political challenges, how citizenship and community prevailed in low-income neighbourhoods. It was no surprise to them when their research findings confirmed that low-income communities facing hardship can, and often do, become stronger and prosper.

Using only open and participatory processes, they gathered 3,000 stories in response to questions such as, "Can you tell us a story about a time when you and your neighbours came together to make things better around here?" The stories they gathered had in common some mix of the six key community building blocks. While not every story was possessed of all six, across the 3,000 stories gathered these are the ones that were most recurrent:

1. The skills of local residents

2. The power of local associations

3. The resources of public, private and non-profit institutions

4. The physical resources and ecology of local places

5. The economic resources of local places

6. The stories and heritage of local places

These building blocks, which John and Jody and their associates eventually categorised as "community assets," reflected the local residents down-to-earth, real-world accounts of their experiences in nurturing their health and wellbeing, protecting the environment and the local economy, raising happy children, aging actively and comfortably at home, responding to natural or man-made disasters, as well as being good stewards of local ecology and of deepening democracy, achieving social justice and nurturing local wisdom.

An understanding of the existence and value of these "community assets" has since served to directly challenge traditional approaches to urban and rural development initiatives that have maintained a focus, by the helping professions, funding agencies and policy makers on the needs and deficiencies of individuals, neighbourhoods, towns, cities and countries.

In their seminal work, *Building Communities from the Inside Out: A Path Toward Finding and Mobilizing a Community's Assets* (1993), John and Jody described in detail this four-year participatory research project and also set down the principles and practices of the asset-based approaches which were informed by their findings.

In essence the book tells us what low-income communities that are becoming stronger do naturally. They use what they have within and around them, get it connected productively and inclusively, and from there secure what they need from outside to ensure their shared future. Encouraged by record sales of the book, John and Jody established the Asset-Based Community Development Institute in 1995.

That year John McKnight published *The Careless Society: Community and Its Counterfeits*, a series of essays written during his 40 years of tireless work in the urban neighbourhoods of Canada and the United States. The book offers a scathing commentary on "how competent communities have been invaded, captured, and colonised by professionalized services," and spells out the devastating results of this colonisation. He also presents an unrivalled exposition on the capacity of communities to resolve many of the escalating social problems that they face.

Over the proceeding 15 years (1995 – 2010), a range of hands-on workbooks and other publications on applying an asset-based approach around the world has been produced by the staff and faculty members of the ABCD Institute.

In 2010, John McKnight and Peter Block collaborated on a book entitled *Abundant Community: Awakening the Power of Families and Neighborhoods*. In it they argue that, as well as needing a village to raise a child, a village is also the key to a satisfying and fulfilled life for everyone else across the life course. The book reminds us that we need our connections with neighbours and community to stay healthy and productive, to protect the land and to take care of ourselves, our young, our old and those on the margins. This book adds a deeper reflection on the role of families and personal efficacy than was contained in previous publications.

Since work began in 1969, the archives are now replete with practical tools and probing analyses of modern society. Taken in the round, they offer both a proscription and prescription of modern society.

The *proscription*: don't seek your good life in the marketplace; it will make you sick.

The *prescription*: in each of our neighbourhoods reside those, whose gifts and talents can produce almost all that we need to live well and to prosper, if we can discover, connect and mobilise them into productive and inclusive action.

Today, the ABCD Institute and the principles and processes that it espouses occupy a central position in a large and growing international social movement, which affirms local "community assets" as the primary building blocks of sustainable community empowerment and development.

In 2014, ABCD Europe was formally established, after operating informally since 2010, which is formally affiliated with the ABCD Institute. There are also ABCD networks in Oceania, Africa and Asia and of course across North America supported by the ABCD in Action Network.

Coady International Institute, and Bank of I.D.E.A.S., based in Australia (and operating worldwide) have also been leaders across the Global South and beyond in promoting an asset-based community development approach.

With this rich history and the strength of global collaborations rooted in living neighbourhoods across the planet, we invite you to join us in celebrating the last few decades of our efforts, and in hatching the dreams and actions that will become visible in the decades to come.

Section Two: Looking Back

"The people that have most influenced John McKnight's thinking"

Saul Alinsky, photo public domain

Interview One – Saul Alinsky

> *There's power because you've got a lot of money and there's power because you have a lot of people. And we don't have a lot of money in this neighbourhood but we do have a lot of people— they're just not organised to be powerful....yet!*

Cormac Russell (CR): So here I am with Professor John McKnight. It's late September 2013 and we're going to spend the next few days in conversation, talking about the influences and individuals who have inspired John and the ABCD movement. We'll revisit the foundations of ABCD, chatting through the key milestones, lessons learned and visions for the future. For this part of the conversation we're going to start with the key influencers and the inspirers of ABCD.

So, John, it's good to be with you. Our conversations will be free flowing, so let's start with the broad and open question of identifying the key influencers and inspirations for you and ABCD over the years.

John McKnight (JMK): I think that there were three major influences on defining ABCD at the outset. The first was Saul Alinsky in the United States, the inventor of neighbourhood organising of a particular kind. The second was Ivan Illich, a great intellectual, social historian and critic. He was especially well-known in the fifties, sixties and seventies and was a good friend of mine. The third was the fact that in mid-career I went from neighbourhood organising and civil rights activism to life as a Professor at university. I'd say that was the third major determinant.

So to go back and weave those three together, when I was in high school Saul Alinsky published a book called *Reveille for Radicals*. It was a description of his attempts to organise a working-class neighbourhood made up largely of immigrants.

Incidentally, a significant part of that population was Irish—pretty much trampled on by industry and the political machine, and not feeling very powerful in themselves. He wanted to create a power-based organisation that would allow them some influence and leverage with the big institutions.

His concept was that there were two kinds of power: there's power because you've got a lot of money and there's power because you have a lot of people. And we don't have a lot of money in this neighbourhood but we do have a lot of people – they're just not organised to be powerful–yet!

So he brought them together, not so much as individuals but as groups, clubs and institutions. He also drew together their veterans' organisations, their ethnic organisations, their sports clubs – all of the indigenous local groups. Each, in a sense, had a vote in shaping the issues and what the organisation would do.

The organisation's main method was to confront and create conflict with institutions. They set out to get people organised, committed and prepared enough to be willing to march on a factory, or go to city hall and confront the mayor!

So it was conflict-organising: You organise people to create confrontation and conflict with institutions that were usually *outside* the neighbourhood but had control over the neighbourhood. Organised people grew powerful enough in relation to the institutions that they could get to the table and negotiate as powerful equals.

Saul would say, "Get to the table," and what he meant by getting to the table was based on his own earlier experience. He had been associated with a guy, John L Lewis, who was the head of the mineworkers and of the Congress of Industrial Organisations that was organising unions in the steel mills, the automobile factories, the farm equipment factories, all that heavy industry. With Lewis, Saul learned about confronting, and about the methods used by the union organisers. Saul brought these tactics back to a neighbourhood and taught people in a given neighbourhood how to organise. *Reveille for Radicals* describes this process.

This book was a life changer for me. When I was a junior at high school I don't think I had any idea at all of what I might do with my life but when I read *Reveille for Radicals,* I had a *eureka* moment when I realised that this was what I really wanted to do!

CR: Just dig into that a little bit, John. What particular aspects of the book attracted you most?

JMK: I think what attracted me was this—my family were New Deal Democrats, who had a class orientation about society, (they looked at Wall Street and the big bankers and industrialists as the bad guys). I was born in the Depression and in those days people didn't look highly on the big guys that brought us down. I was raised with the idea that big institutions were suppressing everyday people.

And I was living in a small town outside of Toledo, Ohio, a strictly working-class town. Alinsky was talking about the kind of people that I lived with. I don't think it was the method, so much, that attracted me: it was that here was an effective way to change the power between the people who "have" and the people who "have not."

And it was clear that Alinsky wasn't just interested in pacifying the community. He was prepared to use the energy of confrontation to gain results. He knew that a common enemy melded people together, so Saul needed an adversary – a mayor, a plant manager, a director of the transportation system, the supermarket store that sold bad meat.

Enemies unite diverse groups and offer them a common cause. If you can find an outside enemy, you can bring people together, solidify your organisation and create positive relationships that might never happen in the normal course of life because of ethnicity, race, and so on.

All of that was attractive to me, and the fact this was a way for people who were at the bottom, (you have to remember at the time about two thirds of the country, had come out of Depression and the War), to reclaim power and restore it to its rightful place.

Franklin Roosevelt always talked about the "patricians" and the "plutocrats." His domestic politics were based on the proposition that there are a bunch of bad guys and the government has to get control of them – and there's the unions who've got to get control of the bad guys and the government.

Most people I knew thought this way, but what attracted me was that all of that seemed big stuff, presidents and unions. And what Alinsky was talking about was that he was a single organiser in a neighbourhood. It attracted me and I thought that maybe I could be that too. I might not be head of a union or president of the United States, but I could be an organiser. And his book tells about how he organised these people in their neighbourhood and all the things that they were able to achieve, using these confrontation methods. The goal was getting to the table, which was what unions did. When the unions finally got organised and the companies had to recognise them they came to the table to negotiate.

So that's what Alinsky was trying to achieve in a neighbourhood, creating a similar organisation like the unions who could confront institutions with enough power to make the institutions sit down at the table and negotiate. Then there could be some equality of power.

Saul said that nobody ever gave any power away voluntarily, that it's a struggle, and you have to create conflict.

Alinsky did this organising in Chicago and lived in Chicago. And it so happened I got a scholarship to go to Northwestern University in Chicago. That put me in a position where I could get in contact with those who Alinsky was teaching and I became a part of that network. It was mostly young men. Women were not involved as Saul was a complete chauvinist. It was from that network that I got into neighbourhood organising.

My own personal heritage also fuelled this developing interest I had in empowering the community. The McKnights were Reformed Presbyterians. They called themselves Covenanters, and they were extremist Presbyterians. They'd fled from Scotland because the Dragoons came down on the Covenanters and they were thought of as like terrorists against the English people.

They were just working-class people, mostly from the Lowlands, who refused to accept that the King of England could be head of the Church of Scotland. They believed that only Jesus could be head of the Church, and they took that to the bitter end. They were outlawed and held their church services out on the moors, and when the dragoons were sent down to massacre them all, they finally left and went to Northern Ireland. This was in the late 17th century. My grandfather was one of these Covenanters in the early 20th century.

They were suppressed when they got to Ireland and so there aren't many of them left: I think about 4,000 in the United States, maybe 9,000 in Northern Ireland and just a few in Scotland. But, because of their resistance to the Crown, and their unwillingness to go along with the other Presbyterians and give in and compromise, I was raised with the belief that you couldn't trust anybody who had power.

Alinsky provided a solution to this sense of disenfranchisement. However, the core of his ideology was that one would not expect good things to come from big and powerful institutions, whether they are businesses or not-for-profits or government. When I went away to college and then spent some time as an organiser, I had a worldview that there were people in neighbourhoods who, if they were organised, had great potential to become powerful and change this exploitative system. And so you see the people in the neighbourhood have that capacity. Outside the neighbourhood are the exploiters—the institutional leaders. Covenanters believed that. New Deal affirmed that. Saul said, "That's right and here's what you can do to correct that."

CR: And he gave you some practical tools to that end.

JMK: And he gave me practical and personal methods to do something about it.

I was mostly organising in neighbourhoods where it was clear to me that the people there had skill, ability, and perseverance but had also suffered a great deal. I was impressed by their resolution and their life experience. A lot of the organising I did was with black African Americans and many of them had been exploited and discriminated against.

In fact, my direct experience was that here were these really smart people. My mission was to help them create an organisation which would be powerful enough to create institutional change, and utilise all their great qualities.

CR: John, were you studying in college at the same time as you were doing the community organising? What was the chronology of events?

JMK: No, you couldn't study at college and community organise at that time.

CR: You were saying you had a scholarship to go to Northwestern University. Can you tell me about that and how that experience informed your thinking?

JMK: I did major in a subject that was relevant. Northwestern had a College of Speech, which taught public speaking, group discussion, theatre, interpretation, radio, TV. So I majored in Public Speaking and Group Communication.

Group Communication was largely focused on group dynamics. I was involved in a lot of experimentation in the classroom and learning about small groups, how they work and what they could do. I knew this area of research and practice was fundamental in neighbourhood organisations.

CR: Let me ground the discussion again in community practice with this question: How does a community builder viewing the world through an ABCD lens think differently to an Alinsky-style organiser?

JMK: Well, for an Alinksy organiser the main thinking was that power is the ability to get institutions to respond to what you wanted. Maybe they weren't going to do it without conflict, so you had to muster enough people power to create the conflict so that they would come to the table.

So effective Alinsky organising is predicated on local people being a part of two things:

1. Defining what the issues are: Where do we want to go? Who are the people behind the issues that we want to get to?

2. Participating in the process of putting pressure on the institutions by being a large threatening number of people.

So it is your presence as a neighbourhood resident acting collectively with other residents, and confronting institutions, that was your role as a citizen in community organising. You were dealing with institutional issues head on.

Now an ABCD approach would say that that Alinsky "power-organising" is a very important thing to do. However, there's another major part of the community power process – it's what we can organise together to make our life better and solve problems with the assets and resources we already have locally.

The big conceptual difference is that the ABCD community builder would be focused mainly on local residents as creators, producers and problem solvers.

But an Alinsky organiser sees local residents as advocates. We're at war with the enemy, so how many troops can we get together? While the Alinsky organiser focuses outside, the ABCD connector focuses inside. Both are legitimate, but ABCD community building is still in its infancy and Alinsky organising has really reached its limit.

Outside the neighbourhood the other mediums for change are the social services and government-funded programmes. These institutions generally see residents as needing to be fixed and ensures that all the useful resources for doing the fixing come from outside.

Ivan Illich, photo public domain

Interview Two – Ivan Illich

If you let institutions grow, become big and powerful through time, then these are the phases. While they're small they'll be relatively productive and over time as bureaucracy and power are assembled, they begin to become less and less productive. Then they'll begin to decline in productivity until they become counter-productive.

CR: And in the late 60's you met another major influence: Ivan Illich

JMK: Yes, Ivan Illich came into my life.

Not many people know about him today, but between the 1950s and 1970s he was very, very well known. He could draw more people than Bob Dylan to any university campus.

He befriended me and he'd stay at our house whenever he came to the United States; he had a centre called CIDOC (Centro Intercultural de Documentación) in Cuernavaca, Mexico where I regularly attended his seminars. I also became his booking agent for his work in North America. I would go down there and create a seminar and he joined me a couple of times in seminars here. We were very close.

At that time he was writing institutional critiques. For example he wrote a book called *De-schooling Society*, which was a critique of schools. *Medical Nemesis* critiqued the medical system, and *Energy and Equity*, which was a critique of all of the corporate systems that were leading us into high-carbon dependency. He had also written a book which was very critical of the Catholic Church—and he was a Catholic priest himself.

Ivan was the most intelligent, educated man I've ever met in my life. I was able to learn a huge amount from him. Yet, though he was more learned than me, he brought me into his inner circle after hearing me speak and realising we shared a great deal. He was being vocal in his criticism of institutions, and he heard me saying much the same thing. On one occasion we spoke at the same venue and we realised that we had common ground, most specifically in our view that institutions mess up most people, their lives and their communities.

I think another reason he took me, rather than some of his intellectual colleagues into his inner circle, was because he recognised my views were innate and developed by life experiences, rather than by academic learning.

CR: How did that feel, John, as a young man working with someone older?

JMK: Well, he was only about nine years older than me, though he seemed older. I never got over the fact that he was willing to spend time with me. I would be with him down in Mexico with people he had invited from all over the world for a floating four or five days of seminars. I strained to understand what they were talking about because they knew literature, they knew history, and they'd be referring to things I didn't know —theology and all the things that I knew very little about. So I was always learning a huge amount and I'd say I felt honoured.

Ivan's centre in Cuernavaca, Mexico was perhaps the leading place for radicals, radical actors and thinkers at the height of the 60s and 70s.

Now the radical I mean is not like Marxists might be described. Often people think radical means extreme. However, a radical understanding goes to the root: in that sense, an extremist isn't usually a radical. I couldn't have given you a really very sophisticated critique back then, but I was sitting around with people who could, people like Edgar Friedenberg and John Holt and all of the great educational critics. And I learnt in great detail why these institutions that I distrusted were distrustful.

Being with Ivan gave me a very sophisticated understanding of the limits of institutions as the producers of wellbeing.

CR: Did you find that as a result of these thoughtful theoretical frames, issuing from these discussions in Cuernavaca, that you reviewed Alinsky's thinking in a deeper way, maybe even revised it?

JMK: Strange as it may seem, I probably didn't. And I didn't because the common theme of all these intellectuals, Alinsky included, was that you can't trust big institutions. Now I did learn Illich met Alinsky one time, because they were both very notable radicals. Illich felt uncomfortable with Saul because he didn't think creating this kind of conflict was the best way forward.

Now I hesitate as I tell you this because I don't think Illich ever had a very clear activist position. Activists clustered around him because of his thinking, but he would say quite often to me, and to others, that he was willing to define proscriptions but not prescriptions. He would say, "I am doing work that explicates what *not* to do. But I am not telling people what they *should do*. My critiques are saying that all of these institutions are doing things you *shouldn't do*."

I had the shell of an idea about institutions from my Scottish culture and Covenanter ancestry, but I didn't understand the internal mechanics, the structure that made institutional production become so counterproductive. So that's what I learned from Illich.

CR: And if you were to summarise the inner mechanics that make institutional production become counter-productive, what would you say?

JMK: Well, I'd say that scale and time are major factors. Illich would say, beyond a certain "intensity" institutions became counterproductive. I would say beyond a certain scale, time and power, institutions that were created to do something decline in their ability to do that thing.

Illich would draw a "productivity" line moving upward. Then it began to flatten out as time went by. And then the line began to descend. Finally the line would turn backward indicating counter-productivity. They began to produce the opposite of what they were created for.

CR: Iatrogenesis.

JMK: Yes. That was his great definition—doctor-created disease. If you let institutions grow, become big and powerful through time, then these are the phases. While they're small they'll be relatively productive and, as time and bureaucracy and power are assembled, they begin to become less and less productive. Then they'll begin to decline in productivity until they become counterproductive.

So he would talk about crime-making criminal justice systems. Nobody doubts that. We've got this huge prison system in the United States and it is misnamed: it's our National Crime Academy. It's a crime-making criminal justice system. Schools, he said, have become stupid-making schools. And in all the years I was at the university I would say I saw that happen. I was there for 35 years and by the time I left I think what students knew, that a member of a democracy ought to know, had declined to zero and managerial and technological information had engulfed them in techno-stupidity.

CR: So there's an inverse correlation then between techno-stupidity and citizenship and community competence?

JMK: That's right. Illich would talk about dependency creating governance and social service systems. Now, when we first came together, I suppose I had already begun to think a lot about the dependency that I saw created in neighbourhoods: How did it happen that people became that dependent, that non-resistant? I saw this especially in the social service world that surrounded the low-income neighbourhoods I was organising, which treated everybody as though they were deficient.

Government is a major contributor to that, at least in the United States, where the government funds the social service world. The government doesn't do much directly in the United States but it provides an awful lot of money for the not-for-profit institutions. I had written essays about this, called *The Careless Society, a Community and Its Counterfeits*. By "counterfeits", I meant all the things that people with degrees and certifications create in lieu of real community.

A friend put me in touch with a publisher who was interested in publishing these essays. I'm pretty sure that when Illich and I first met, I had already become known for that critique. He'd written a report about schools, and one about energy, and one about the church and medicine, but he hadn't done social services. In a sense that book is a minor version of Illich's thoughts but covers an area he hadn't critiqued. I'm sure that helped open the door.

CR: So he would have seen you as a fellow traveller?

JMK: Yes. I was analysing the world in the same way that he had.

Frank Haiman, used with permission from Northwestern University Archives

Interview Three – Frank Haiman

> *The way to really reform society is to create a society where the people at the edge are inside, not by making new rules and laws that will keep them further outside. Community building is about getting the greatest number of contributions by the greatest number of people.*

CR: Up to this point we've been talking about Alinsky and Illich's influence on your thinking and practice; we've also talked about your journey from neighbourhood organising to civil rights activism to your role as a professor at Northwestern

University. In the next part of our conversation, I'd like to explore general semantics and language, and how that thinking applied to community organising and ABCD as influenced by Frank Haiman.

JMK: As an undergraduate, I was in the School of Speech at Northwestern University. One of the disciplines was called Group Dynamics. It was a big thing at the time. It was an attempt to bring social psychology into the study of small group process. That has been very helpful to me because I left the university and spent a great deal of my life with small groups.

The professor who taught Group Dynamics was Franklin Haiman. He became a very close friend and has been a friend and ally all my life. Frank was a researcher, one of the leading-edge people looking at small group processes – what makes small groups effective and what doesn't.

But he grew more interested in freedom of speech and he became an important figure in the American Civil Liberties Union. It's a national organisation in the US that legally defends the Bill of Rights with lawsuits to expand freedom of speech and freedom of expression. As he moved from Group Dynamics into freedom of speech I sort of moved with him.

Frank was on the board of the Illinois Division of the American Civil Liberties Union (ACLU). They had an opening for an executive director. Frank put my name in the hopper and I got the job. And in that position I had a great learning opportunity about liberty and rights. People were walking in my door all the time saying they had been denied some right or liberty that was protected by the constitution. There I learned a lot about dissent because almost everybody that the government was coming down on was in some way a dissenter.

The government might have been coming down on them because they were a communist, or authors whose writing had been deemed obscene. They might be people who were picketing, or demonstrating, all the forms of expression across the political spectrum.

So I was dealing with these people who were almost always marginal. That was a huge learning experience for me because it let me see who is at the edge of society and that the way to really reform society is to create a community where the people at the edge are inside, not making new rules and laws that will keep them further outside.

One of the things that influenced me in that regard was that we defended many people who were pretty eccentric and today would be called extremists. The thing that really struck me about all these dissenters was that all of them were expressing their belief and the government was coming down on them. Yet the government action never changed a single one of them.

It's hopeless to try changing people by denying them the right to express themselves. Freedom of expression is critical in a democratic society. I believe in the importance of people at the margins, something which became clear later in my life through the ABCD effort. We've been particularly concerned to recognise that the people at the edge are assets and that if we can offer them an opportunity to participate, then society becomes stronger and their hopes are fulfilled rather than repressed.

A fair amount of what ABCD has meant in practice is focused on people at the margins becoming active participants and producers in the community. And this is Jerry Miller's (who we'll speak about later) principle: If you start at the edge and get those folks involved, it's all easy from there, because these people are the hardest people for others to accept.

The perspective I found at the ACLU and with Frank Haiman manifested itself in the idea that a strong community is one in which everybody contributes, and that the fewer people who contribute the weaker the community will be. Therefore, at its baseline, community building is about getting the greatest number of contributions by the greatest number of people.

Those least likely to be contributing are the people at the margin and for me a real ABCD person is one who is very much aware that the human beings least likely to be understood as having capacity and skill, are those at the margin. They are usually easily identified because they are given labels – indeed I tend to call them "labelled people." They're people labelled not around their gifts but around perceived deficiencies, the "developmentally disabled," "the welfare recipients," the "ex-convicts," the "youth at risk," the "mentally ill." All those words are ways of telling a community that the important thing about these people is not that they are an asset, but that they have defects.

So the primary asset from an asset-based perspective is the gifts and the capacities of the individuals. It is the No. 1 thing. Once you can see what the world is like from the edge rather than the centre, then you have a completely different understanding. That's why I think ABCD should always be focused on maximising contributions, inviting those at the edge inside because we need them if we want to be strong.

Robert Mendelsohn, photo public domain

Interview Four – Robert Mendelsohn

Bob's books should be read by every doctor who wants to know what they can do that's respectful and not disabling of communities' power to be healthful and of family power to do healthful things.

CR: So let's talk about Bob Mendelsohn.

JMK: Bob Mendelsohn was a doctor who lived here in Evanston where I live and I must have met him here in the 60s.

When **Head Start** (Head Start is a program of the United States Department of Health and Human Services that provides comprehensive early childhood education, health, nutrition, and parent involvement services to low-income children and their families) began he was a very prominent paediatrician and they made him the Medical Director of Head Start— "The nation's paediatrician." He held that position for a while, but because he was too radical or because Head Start was too bureaucratic, he left.

He began to write books, a nationally syndicated newspaper column, a newsletter, and appeared on television and radio programmes on a regular basis. His first book was called *The Confessions of a Medical Heretic*. You can still get it and I highly commend it.

From his experience as a paediatrician he became convinced that the medical professions were taking over people's lives, "medicalising them" to such an extent that the patients were not in control of their lives, or their health.

People were turning ever more to professionals for something that they should be dealing with through their community and through their family. When people would come in and sit down in his office and describe what was wrong he'd say to them, "What would your grandmother have done about that?" Bob said that's the way he learned how to be an effective doctor. He was a board-certified, famous paediatrician yet that was the primary question that he asked.

Bob had a very strong belief that healthful knowledge lay in the community and that medicine was stealing the "health" from local communities. Of course that's how I came to know him, and we wrote some articles together for various medical journals.

I began to see that his assault on medicine as a practising doctor was what a responsible professional would do. He was always struggling with that belief that doctors were medicalising people.

Bob felt that doctors had taken over women's lives, medicalised them. So he wrote a book called *Male Practice* but, it was printed to look like it said "Malpractice" because the "e" of "male" was just an outline!

He thought the Obstetrics & Gynaecology (Obs & Gynae) world had taken over women's lives. Pregnancy was dealt with in the sickness idiom and breastfeeding was one of God's many mistakes: you shouldn't breastfeed because the paediatricians and the Obs & Gynae medics said formula was superior—that was the official position of the American Pediatric Association in those days. So he was fighting that too. Bob was an ally of Marion Thompson, founder of La Leche League International, in the fight against formula supplanting breast milk. He was a medical authenticator for that movement.

He was also the paediatrician for my children but that was not saying a lot, because he didn't believe paediatricians were much help for children. In watching him with my children and listening to him talking, reading his books and interacting with him, I could see how he had fashioned his way to become a respectable and respectful professional practitioner.

His third book is called *How to Raise a Healthy Child In Spite of Your Doctor*. It's still out there. Bob's books should be read by every doctor who wants to know what they can do to support communities, and families, to behave in healthful ways.

Bob was a professional trying to answer the same question as me, at the opposite end: What am I really needed for?

Just as Jerry Miller (see interview six, page 49) was the most humane public official I've ever met, Bob Mendelsohn was the most humane health professional I've ever met. His books helped lay people and medical people re-orient their functions and relationships with each other. Bob was saying that doctors keep acting as if they can do something powerful, scientific and curative that keeps people from doing the real thing that needs to be done – the radical thing that needs to be done by them, their families and their communities.

His books provided an alternative to a medical approach which resulted in patients being prescribed barbiturates and tranquilisers rather than addressing the problems in their families or community.

CR: One of the things that strikes me is there was once a lot of talk in the UK, about co-production: it's one of these terms that's got broken off from the radical root and has become something in itself. But most of what people write about in relation to co-production, is professionally-led activity. It focuses on relationships with individuals with particular labels. So essentially it's about service co-design not co-production of democracy or a good life in general terms. I think that's what's radical about Bob's work: he's talking about the limits of the professional and the systems around him, and the capacities of the citizen and the community around here, which is a very different frame, I think, from a lot of the co-production stuff.

JMK: Many people, including people in ABCD, use the word "co-production." I'm personally pretty hesitant about that for exactly the reason you mention.

Rather than talk about co-production I would ask about the appropriate roles and functions of experts. What's needed to avoid harm is for professionals to conduct a neighbourhood impact statement, like an environmental impact statement.

You could as local residents have a community impact statement for professionals, and you and your neighbours could say before you can intervene as a professional, we'd like to lead you through a process of looking at the community impact of what you're going to do – like how many grandmothers' knowledge and roles will be displaced by what you do? That's Bob Mendelsohn's teaching.

I do believe there is a place and a space for experts, but I don't think about it as co-production. Co-production in my mind is people from systems wanting to talk about respect for community people. But in 90% of the cases I think it is a ritual rather than a reality.

It's a ritual no matter how hard professionals try because they have all the money, they have the power, they have the white coat, they have the certificate on the wall, and they have an institution behind them.

And I as an individual, or even my neighbourhood group, have very little of the kind of muscle the professional has. Measured by muscle there is no real "co" in most co-production.

If, on the other hand, you say communities and citizens are the principal producers of wellbeing, that is a good idea.

The idea should be that the centre of life is the community and the productive citizens. Then the question is: Can experts be of help?

When can experts be of help rather than controlling, redefining and evaluating?

CR: So the citizen is the landlord and the professional, the servant.

JMK: Bob Mendelsohn could tell you what he thought was legitimate action that a professional might take because he had done a community impact analysis of himself.

All of his books said, in essence, here's all the stuff that we do in the name of health that actually isn't healthy or helpful—it's iatrogenic.

In the latter days, when Bob became renowned for being a radical doctor, I asked him who were the patients who came to see him.

He said, "I'm the last stop of people who have problems before they go to Lourdes."

They hoped that finally there was some medical expert who could help them because they'd been through all the rest.

CR: Living out the Hippocratic oath…

JMK: Yes, "do no harm,"—that's the top of the list. *Do no harm*. Bob was serious about that. Many of the doctors I deal with see that the whole medical system, the pill system, the hospital system—is now out of their control and is controlled by people who understand systems and making money.

CR: That's my experience as well. Last week I was speaking to a clinical commissioner for dementia: his job is to figure out with all the other doctors in the county what they ought to do about dementia, and he said, "We're stumped, we are stumped. We can't do this without community, this is not purely a clinical issue, this is largely outside our sphere of influence."

JMK: My mother lived in a little town in Ohio, about 17,000 people. When I was about 40 I was introduced to the field of developmental disabilities and began doing some work with the progressives in that field, on how to get people with that label back into community life.

So when I went home to my mother in her little town, and I told her that I had begun to work with people in this group. She asked what developmental disabilities are. I didn't use the word "retarded" because I'd learned from the people with developmental disabilities that's a bad word.

So I tried to describe some aspects of them: that they're people who are born with uncommon limits, who may never read much or count money and some may not walk too firmly and sometimes their faces don't look like other people's faces.

So when she knew what I meant, she said, "Oh I know them, but now they're all gone."

It was the 1960s and I asked what she meant. And she said, "Well, those kinds of people used to be around here all the time. But I think since the Second World War they've all gone."

What she meant was that these were people who were part of her life when she was a young woman in this town but something began to happen during and after the war to change that. I asked where she thought they'd gone. She said, "I don't know, I've never thought about it. They used to be here and now they're not."

"These people" had been institutionalised. That's not to say they weren't institutionalised in the past but not nearly as many. So I asked, "Who has gone?"

"Well, like Billy Wheeler. He was the Wheelers' son and he couldn't really go to school. But he worked at the *Daily Globe* and he wrapped the newspapers up with string in batches for the boys who came in to deliver them."

And she began to describe to me how, in her youth, "developmentally disabled" people were active and had a role and function in this little community of 17,000 people.

And in the 1960s John O'Brien a leading progressive in the field, asked us, "How can we get these people back in communities?"

Well, if I'd been smarter than I am I would have suggested to John we go talk to my mother. She came from a world of people who knew how to live with neighbours who are now labelled as deviant.

That's not to say that everything was hunky dory in community life back then. There were terrible abuses going on side by side with the good stuff. But still, in most communities people that would now be called disabled, senile or developmentally disabled, had a place and a function. So if I wanted to know what to do with any class of people that are labelled, the first thing I'd do is go back and look at how marginalised people were included in community life.

Bad things happened and continue to happen but good things in the community were happening too. We don't have to reinvent it; we can rediscover it.

CR: And rediscovery is at the heart of ABCD, isn't it? This recognition that we're not bringing anything new, that it's there already –perhaps hidden and disconnected, but there. We just have to rediscover.

JMK: That's right. A word I'd use that seems appropriate to me is *invisible*. What ABCD does for most people is to make visible all the resources that surround them.

CR: Do you know the Sufi story? I've taken it and Irishified it! Father Murphy wakes up one night, and he puts on his trousers and in the process his house keys fall out of his trouser pocket and under his bed. And then he's standing outside his front door under his porch light and searching, you see. And Mary, the lady who looks after the sacristy passes by and on seeing Father Murphy, says, "Aw! Father Murphy, how are you?" And he says, "I'm not well, Mary. I've lost my keys." She says, "I can see you're looking for something. Where did you lose them, Father?" He says "I lost them up under the bed, Mary." And she says, "Well, what are you doing out here, Father?" He says, "I can't see a blooming thing under the bed, Mary! At least there's light out here."

And that's the corollary, isn't it? We're looking for solutions in well-lit places, instead of revealing the invisible all around us.

JMK: ABCD is the light that shines under the bed. I like that. Perfect!

CR: The systems look for the solutions in the well-lit places and they're actually under the bed in the murky, messy, dark, out-of-control and more ordinary places.

JMK: Right. One thing I would want to add which really comes through strongly for me from my work with Illich is that we are not saying that everything can be done within the realm of the relationships of community.

We will always fail to be God. I'm writing an essay called "The Incredible Possibilities of Failing to be God." The professionals are trying to be God.

If we stopped believing in professionals we would have incredible possibilities because we could say professionals aren't God and we could give them permission to say, "We aren't gods, stop expecting us to be. We can't do it!"

We might say that recognising this is a part of the culture of community. And the most obvious personal limit is that we have pain and suffer, and we die.

And this is a physiological question. We are in pursuit of killing pain and suffering and failure. One way of looking at the absurdity of modernism is to say that's what it is about, and look at the consequences.

The alternative is to say we fail, and we have pain and suffering but as a community we have ways to deal with that.

Together we mourn. We cry with each other. We have a party at the time of death. We come together and remember Charles every Saturday night. These are community rituals that recognise suffering and pain and death.

Like any institution, at Northwestern University where I worked, they didn't know what to do about death because they're all about being

God.

And so it always amused me—a faculty member who was an important influence died, we would get a little white card from the President's office saying there will be a memorial service for Charlie at the chapel at two o'clock on Wednesday afternoon. That's it.

So that's the institutional solution to his widow's problems, his friends' problems, his colleagues' problems—a little white, mass-produced card, just change the name and send it out every time someone passes.

CR: Later we'll also talk more about the limits of local. There's an organisation whose tagline is "There are no limits to local." And of course there are. It seems to me to be a salient point.

JMK: Yes, it is. I believe we can't really be very creative and problem solving in the community until we abjure the claims of technology and systems to solve every problem. Because the more they over reach, the more problems they create.

One of the most helpful things that I learned from Illich is that progress depends on understanding limits. And if you don't, you'll begin to act like God. And the Greeks knew about that: it's called hubris.

CR: Jean Vanier had the wonderful observation that you cannot truly commit to community until you've become disenchanted by it.

JMK: Ah, that's very, good. Bob Mendelsohn understood the limits of a doctor. And everything has limits, so communities do too.

CR: It's the fundamental joy of humanity—fallibility. And in a sense isn't it true to say that when fallibility and assets are thought about together they make sense of each other, because if we only think about assets, there is a real risk of hubris, a real

risk that we get reduced to the positive psychology section of the library, instead of the political section.

JMK: I like to point out that I don't want to be romantic about communities—as local communities can be murderous. Look what happened in former Yugoslavia when the dictator left, and the ethnic communities resurfaced. People who had lived together almost a hundred years in peace killed their next-door neighbours.

CR: And Rwanda, the same.

JMK: One tribe against the other.

CR: So many examples of that.

JMK: This is a real dilemma. Some sociologists say community is a word for a group of people who believe they are specially related, have an affinity, but by that very act they create outsiders. That is a profound thought.

I once belonged to the Cook County Labrador Retriever Owner Association because we just loved our lab. We'd all go out once a month and meet in a park and bring our dogs. We'd talked together about how wonderful our dogs were and the dogs sniffed each other.

That was it—the joy of association.

And then one day out of the woods into the parking lot came a woman with a wonderful German Shepherd dog, and all of a sudden the question is whether we want to let her in? What holds us together is the belief that we have the best breed of dog in the world.

That belief seems innocent, lovely, warm, and relational. It's good. But it is?

Judith Snow's (see interview seven pg. 57) answer is that we must always work hard to keep a welcome at the edge of a community, and that means we have to create a culture of hospitality. Therefore the basic act of community is welcoming. This welcome is in the interests of labelled and non-labelled people alike.

Robert Rodale, photo public domain

Interview Five – Robert Rodale

The way the natural world works is an example and a metaphor for the way that community works. Some farmers in the United States would come and chop down all the trees and then mono-crop the land... In a sense, they'd created a desert. But nature has a strategy for recovering that land... At first, a group of fast-growing plants with big leaves appear. Then, a second layer of plants grows: they need shade and some protection from the first layer until they grow bigger than the first plants. And there's a natural succession in which recovery of the land takes place, until finally great trees appear – they're the ultimate expression of the recovery.

CR: So John, that brings us to Robert Rodale. Can you tell us about Robert and how he influenced your thinking and ABCD work in general?

JMK: Robert Rodale, and his father J. I. Rodale, really got the organic movement started in the United States. They were big on the relationship between composting, chemical-free horticulture and health.

They started two very popular magazines, one called *Prevention* which was a non-medical approach to health and the other, *Organic Gardening* which was a guide to gardeners on how to garden without destructive chemicals.

So Bob and his father were national leaders of the organic movement and absolutely against all the pesticides and poisons that are put on plants.

I met Bob Rodale through Illich, who'd invited him to one his gatherings. We became close friends. We had many wonderful discussions. He wrote an editorial in every issue of *Organic Gardening* and in several he mentioned the discussions we'd had and the conclusions we'd come to. But I would say that what he did for me was to keep reminding me that the way the natural world works is an example and a metaphor for the way that community works.

A lot of our discussions brought together what I knew about neighbourhoods and what he knew about plants, ecology and environment and how each influenced the other. Up until that time I'd only focused on what I would call the socio-economic space of neighbourhoods. I'd never thought about that space in terms of it being underpinned by the land. It was Bob that brought that into my thinking.

One of the most significant things he told me about was that early farmers in the United States would come and chop down all the trees and then mono-crop the land with wheat year after year after year.

If you did that even on relatively good land you'd find that after thirty or forty years the land would produce hardly any wheat because you'd taken all the nutrients out (that was one of the reasons the Rodales were big on composting, not chemicals). In a sense, you'd created a desert.

What really caught my imagination was when he said nature has a strategy for recovering that land in its very design. I presume that biologists know about this.

At first, a group of fast-growing plants with big leaves appear. Then a second layer of plants grows. They need shade and some protection until they grow bigger than the first plants. And there's a natural succession in which recovery of the land takes place, until finally great trees appear. They are the climax of the recovery process. So he called them Climax Forests – they're the ultimate expression of the recovery.

Bob led me to think a lot about the succession process by which a neighbourhood could be recovered.

What is the first growth?

What would be the second?

And how could the second growth promote the third?

At this time in my life it's probably the recovery process that I am most interested in because most neighbourhoods in the United States and in Canada are not places of connected people. To call them a community would be wrong: a community is a group of related people, but for the most part these people are not really related at all.

But they're there, and you could say that they all came from a history of families and communities, ethnic groups, racial groups, tribal groups, that were once connected—but that the world marketplace has done them in, just as Monsanto has done in the land. And so now their lives are a desert too. What is it that will enable succession in human communities?

Whatever brief time I have left here in this world, will be about experimenting and examining that process.

On our website, www.abcdinstitute.org, there's a little publication called "Exemplary Materials." It's an initial effort to define the first order of recovery from which the second could grow.

So that's Bob Rodale. He was both a very humble man and a very wealthy man. He had great wealth but he lived in the bungalow in which he was born. He gave quite a bit of money to universities to establish their agricultural schools' professorships in organic horticulture, because in the United States a lot of the money that went into agricultural schools came from the chemical companies, (such as the Dows and the Monsantos), who wanted agricultural departments to push their technology.

So he encouraged growth in the scientific world as well as in farming and gardening and discouraged us from letting the market ruin the land.

And he wanted us to learn how we could make change with our own hands and our own development of composting, replenishing the land with a succession of homegrown produce.

CR: Is he still alive?

JMK: No, it's very sad. When the Soviet Union collapsed, he went there to try to start a publication like his own *Successful Farming*, but in Russian. They did chemical farming more than the United States did.

He began to get a publication and a movement going to push organic farming there. But the second time he was there, he was on his way to the airport to come home and a Russian military vehicle went out of control and struck his car head on: everyone in his car was killed. I suppose he might have been 50, so he could have carried on his work for many more years. A great and humble man, very influential.

CR: Thank you for sharing that, John. When I worked with the folks in the permaculture movement in Portugal they shared a very similar observation about nature's ways and cycles of recovery being closely aligned to human communities' recovery cycles. It's really powerful to be reminded that nature is our most important teacher.

JMK: It really helped me to understand that in the neighbourhood I was concerned about, I'd ignored the most basic asset – the land. So in our five assets, the land is right there.

Jerome Miller, used without permission. Credit David Scull

Interview Six – Jerome Miller

Putting them in a Reformatory is the worst thing you could do to prevent kids from being recidivists. At its best it was still the worst thing. And so he came to realise that all this institutional reform misses the point. Radical thinking gets beyond institutional reform. Jerry decided that the reformatory was the worst of all possible solutions and he closed down the state's reformatories one by one, very quickly.

CR: The next person you mentioned as having a huge influence on you is Jerome Miller.

JMK: Jerry Miller was a professor of social work at the Ohio State University, and a very creative person.

He had a lot of ideas about reforming penitentiaries and reformatories for youth, but he was an academic. The State of Massachusetts had eleven reformatories for young people. Some newspapers exposed how cruel and brutal they were. If kids ran away they'd break their fingers or put them in a hole as a penalty when they came back—all kinds of terrible things.

So the governor at the time decided he really needed to bring in somebody to reform the whole system. They interviewed all kinds of people and Jerry Miller decided that, although he'd never run anything before, he would apply.

The governor was so taken with Jerry's radical ideas that he appointed him as head of the juvenile correction system in Massachusetts, including these 11 reformatories and, I guess, some other youth programmes.

Then Jerry introduced the best practices from the field of criminology —those that made decent, respectable, even good reformatories. He brought in many psychologists and professionals and did away with any brutality. He strongly sanctioned anyone working there who was doing harmful things to the kids.

He did that for two years and the reformatories in Massachusetts became the best in the United States.

Looking at the annual report for the second year, he decided to check out the recidivism rate for kids during the brutal system and compare it with the rate now that they had emerged from a "good" system. The rate was about the same.

All of the professionalising hadn't changed the reality for kids very much.

It's wonderful the way he describes this in his book *Last One Over the Wall*. It's one of the most influential books I could recommend for anyone to read.

Jerry said he couldn't figure out anything else he could do that would make a better reformatory. It was then that it occurred to him that maybe even at its best, a reformatory is the worst thing you could do to prevent kids from being recidivists. At its best, it was still the worst thing. Now we're beginning to hear echoes in practice of Ivan Illich's institutional counterproductivity.

Jerry came to realise that all this institutional reform missed the point. Radical thinking gets beyond institutional reform. And that's something that I learned in spades from Jerry Miller.

Having decided that the reformatory was the worst of all possible solutions, he closed down the state's reformatories one by one, very quickly. And that's what Jerry's book *Last One Over the Wall* is all about.

He started with the kids who were thought to be the worst. Initially, he went to the University of Massachusetts, and persuaded the administration to let these kids become room-mates of college students and live with them. And then the college students would begin to know them and think about what good things they could do together with these kids.

Back then the reformatories were spending maybe $27,000 USD per annum per kid. If you decided to use the money differently you had huge purchasing power. Therefore, if you had plausible alternatives to offer there were significant dollars for implementation.

Jerry said to community organisations and agencies, "I'll pay you to think of something to do with these kids that isn't incarceration." And he promoted invention across all sectors of the society, by asking how we might get these kids recovered and reconnected in communities.

He is the most radical public administrator I have ever met in any field in the United States. Every public administrator should have to read *Last One Over the Wall.*

There are a million stories about the non-incarcerating things you might do with a kid if you had some resources. He didn't necessarily have ideas about what these things ought to be, but he dangled his money and gave college kids the challenge of invention.

That's what we should be doing right across the board in all areas. School reform for example is a failure in the United States. We should be saying to communities, "Could you educate these children?"

I don't want to go further into this because anyone can read *Last One Over the Wall,* but there are two stories Jerry told me that were most significant in my mind.

At the time Jerry closed the reformatories, Pan American Airlines was one of the United States' international airlines. At that time, Pan Am offered a "round the world" ticket with which you could start in New York and keep flying west—to San Francisco, then Hawaii, Tokyo, and then Bangkok and on around the world. The ticket was good for a year to make a round the world trip.

You could stop at 50 or 20 or 4 places. As I recall, the ticket was about $3,000, which was very expensive then. One of the college students knew about the Pan Am offer and he said to Jerry, "The two of us (the kid from the reformatory that had become his room-mate at University) want to go around the world in a year and go to all these places and it will cost $3,000 for each of our tickets, so that's $6,000.We think if you gave us another $5,000 that would be all the cash we need—we won't live high or stay in great hotels! So for $11,000, we'll be out of your hair, going round the world."

Jerry said yes. And so they flew around the world and the kid came back a new person, as did the college student!

What Jerry did is the most radical proof of the potential of communities if you free people from the institutional system and promote radical thinking.

Unfortunately, Jerry's reforms didn't spread very much. Every "progressive" reformatory leader in the country was opposed to it, because they would be redundant if there weren't children in "need" of their services.

Jerry came to Illinois and he did the same thing for kids who were not in reformatories but in institutions and group homes because they'd been labelled "abandoned", "neglected" or "abused". He developed a whole set of alternatives for them.

So Jerry made clear to me that Illich was right. Institutions start out doing something constructive and then they level out, decline and then reverse themselves and become crime-making reformatories. People who want to reform reformatories are therefore the great misguiders of society. The progressives, the institutional reformers are the final defenders of keeping what doesn't work going—or as Mike Green would say, "They've never figured out that doing more of what doesn't work won't finally work."

Being involved with Jerry and seeing how he thinks, was the most practical, applied radical experience I've ever had. It also affirmed every idea that I had, that Illich had and others like us had.

CR: That's powerful. And where is he today?

JMK: He retired and lived in a small town in Western Virginia. I visited him there. He's written a couple of other books, especially documenting the devastating effect on black communities of our national system of racist imprisonment.

Supposing a superintendent of schools had thought like Jerry and said, "My job is to close down the school. In this community of 90,000 people, we have a bunch of young people who we want to be effective, productive citizens at the age of 18. I'm spending $8,000 a year on educating each of these kids within the system and it's not working, so let's become a learning community instead."

School reform would dissolve in a day if somebody did that.

Effectively, a lot of the pro-health people are doing that. Cormac, you and I had lunch yesterday with Marion Thompson, the founder of La Leche League International. She told us she had recently gone to a doctor, and she really felt bad about it. I asked why. She said, "Well, I'm 83 and I haven't gone to a doctor for 26 years. It is how I keep healthy: it's not going to a doctor that keeps you well, it's what you do."

Here's another story that I think illustrates the other great lesson Jerry's work provides us. Even at the height of his career he was not the world's greatest administrator but still he was doing all kinds of creative things all over the place. He'd got all these kids out of the reformatories, and involved them all in figuring out what they were going to do next.

He had two rules:

> 1. Start with those who are deepest within the system—the most disempowered, the most disabled, the most violent. If you can show that you can do better for them outside the institution then it's all downhill after that. He didn't do what most people do and "cream off " the people who are the least problematic.

> 2. You never make a plan, because that in itself will stop you. Those in power—officials, professionals, unions—will learn

what you're going to do when they see the plan and because they'll be against it they will mobilise the forces that want to keep the system going the way it is. So act quickly and then act in a way that mobilises the community's resources.

Those are his two rules.

Incidentally, Jerry's great enemy was the "out of sight, out of mind" phenomenon: once the kids were behind the wall they're out of people's minds. You can brutalise them, break their fingers, do whatever you want to them. You've got huge crimes going on inside the walls but nobody knows. Yet society thinks everything's okay. When you let them out, and one of them gets connected to an abusive guy and it gets discovered that there's something untoward going on, the professionals and institutions will jump on it and get it on the front pages of the papers. So that every time you work in the community, your failure is public. Every time you work in the system, the brutality is private. And that's the difference.

So Jerry Miller's greatest problem was those situations. Say he has got 80 kids out of this reformatory and he's got them in all kinds of settings doing all kinds of things. Often those aren't going to work, whereas before, none of them were going to work. But the fact of some of them not working is so publicly visible, creates a demand for "caring institutions" to step in.

We need to have tolerance for those things that don't work in a community setting and instead of exiling these people, putting them behind some wall; we need to have a humane, alternative approach.

Jerry Miller is the most humane professional I've ever met in my life because he said that the best he could have done for the kids in those reformatories was the worst thing that could happen to them.

And in that honesty he created the greatest of the alternatives, better lives for kids.

One other story about Jerry: when he was completely involved in getting these kids out of the reformatories, he forgot about the employees still at the institutions. After a month he got a call from the warden at the reformatory where there had been no kids for a month. The warden says, "Hey, Jerry, I want you to come out here, we need to talk."

Jerry hadn't really thought about what was going on at the reformatory. So a day or two later, he went out and walked into the warden's office and asked "How has it been going?" And the warden tells him "It's never been better!" He had the time cards for every employee who worked in the reformatory and he laid them in front of Jerry and said, "You can check yourself; the workers have been here every day."

A sad fact is that the biggest opponent of serious reform in our prison system is the guards' union. They're very powerful. Jerry Miller was their greatest enemy. And I feel for them. So any real alternative to institutions needs to have a plan for what you're going to do with these people whose unproductive lives are taken apart vocationally.

The biggest consequence of moving to a community alternative is that a lot of people lose their jobs. Here, there is a need for a plan that will find new jobs in some productive sectors.

Then, will the last one over the wall please turn out the lights?

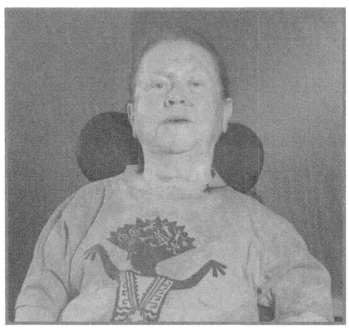

Judith Snow, Screen capture from interview courtesy of the Royal Ontario Museum

*Interview Seven – Judith Snow**

We never have the foggiest idea what people need until we give them those unique resources that allow them to be an active part of the community making their own choices. Then we'll see what they need of us.

CR: You probably know this quote by Upton Sinclair, a great iconoclast and journalist by trade. He said, "A man will never understand that which his salary depends on him not understanding."

JMK: Excellent. You could start this whole part of the book with that quote! Can I add one other example that goes with this? We're talking about a radical understanding of the institutional problem. Judith Snow was also a great influence on me.

Judith is primarily an artist. She is also someone that many have labelled throughout her life. She was born with a capacity to physically do very little with her body. As Judith says: "As a baby, I had full strength for a baby. But my strength never grew with me, so now I can feel everything and move very, very little." She lives her life using a wheelchair and needs 24-hour attendance to enable her to participate.

So in a professional world, they would label her as totally and vocationally disabled. They'd have a whole set of labels for her, portraying her as totally incompetent.

Nonetheless she led the fight in Canada to get labelled people income instead of services. And with her circle of support that she built around herself she became the first person in the Province of Ontario to get an annual personal budget from the government—$120,000—to use for her own wellbeing.

Now she also is a wonderful speaker and trainer and enabler, so she makes money that way too. And as she has to have round-the-clock support, she needs more money than most people.

After she had been on a personal budget, rather than a social service, for two or three years I remember asking Judith: "Tell me how many services for a disabled person you have used in the last year? Because you are now the empirical proof of what is needed as against what professionals say you need."

And she said: "In the last year I have used two services that are unique to me. And one of them I didn't want. So the first one was my very complex wheelchair. I have it because I don't walk so it's related to my disability and so I went to a company of mechanics who understand wheelchair technology and I went to them because I needed them.

"The second service was that every time I want to go somewhere on an airplane, they insist I talk to their disability specialist. I don't need them but I have to deal with them in order to get on an airplane. But as regards all the services that I was dependent on before, I've used none."

And this is a woman who is as physically dependent as you could possibly be.

So if you looked at her you'd think she might need a whole lot of compensatory stuff. But all the system did was justify itself by saying she needed this complex set of services, when what her life demonstrated was that mostly, she didn't.

The service system needs her. She doesn't need it.

The Careless Society: Community and Its Counterfeits is pretty critical of the service system, so when people say to me, "Well, don't you think there is some place for systems?" my answer is yes, but only after so-called "clients" have adequate income.

Systems must be prepared to first say, "You're going to have the income to make all the choices you need to make a regular life." (That's what Judith's income allowed her to do).

We never have the foggiest idea what special services people need until they have those unique resources that allow them to be an active part of the community so they can make their own choices. Then we'll see what services they really need of us.

Judith is the best proof of that. As far as she's concerned she rarely uses specialised services. Yet in the whole architecture of service institutions, she's the poster child of neediness! So she is the great living proof that the huge edifice of specialised services is largely not needed by many labelled people. What they need is what everyone needs: adequate income, access to an everyday community and the relationships they create there, and, of course, choice.

Systems focused on people who are labelled are an alternative to choice. They say, "Your choice is us. We control the money and we run the zoo and you're living in it."

Judith and Jerry taught me so much about thinking radically. I learnt that kids were made bad by "great" reformatories and people were made disabled by disability services.

Here is a list that Judith wrote to remind us of the gifts and assets that people who are vulnerable to rejection commonly bring to community:

Hospitality
Making people feel happy
Listening
Providing a home (to the personal assistant)

Grounding
Slowing people down, reorienting people to time and place
Helping people appreciate simple things
Helping people appreciate their own abilities

Skill-building
Pushing people to be better problem solvers
Causing people to try things they've never done before
Causing people to research things they've never encountered before

Networking
Reaching out to people and breaking down barriers
Asking questions that everyone else is too shy to ask
Bringing people together who otherwise would never meet

Economic

Providing jobs to people who want supplemental income, like artists
Providing jobs to people who need to work odd schedules like homemakers
Providing jobs to people who otherwise have few or no marketable skills

Emotional/Spiritual
Often very forgiving
Often loving and inspiring love
Offering opportunities to do something that clearly makes a difference
Reorienting values from successes to relationships.

Judith goes on to say: "Individuals have unique gifts and they may not have all of the above common gifts. Nevertheless people often privately mention receiving these gifts after getting to know someone labelled "disabled". Imagine if we went public about them and intentionally built these gifts into everyday life."

Jody Kretzmann, screen capture from recorded interview by Goldin Institute

Stan Hallett, photo public domain

Interview Eight – Jody Kretzmann and Stan Hallett

A grant is money that starts big and at the end there is no money. An asset is the opposite of a grant. It starts small and, if you invest it well, it ends up big. It's a multiplier of what people have, from something little to something bigger, not huge but bigger. And so that's why we called them assets. They are the local investments that, correctly connected, will create much more together than they do apart.

CR: How did the research you conducted between 1969 and the late 1980s inform Asset-Based thinking?

JMK: So the set the scene, it's the late 80's, I'm in a research institution and I have around me some brilliant, committed young academics. My colleagues at the Center for Urban Affairs when I first got there were:

Ray Mack

Jody Kretzmann

Fred Du Bow

Tom Dewar

Art Lyons

Alice Murray

Stan Hallett

Andrew Gordon

Paul Arntson

Malcolm Bush

Denis Detzel

I thought the neighbourhood research that I could initiate, (research that wasn't happening in any other policy or urban research centre in the country), wouldn't be about what *wasn't* there – the needs, but would be about what *was* there – the basic resources that were present.

Nobody was doing that. It occurred to me that if I could initiate research to identify the resources people use, it could change policy views and, more importantly, tell local neighbourhood organisers and organisations how people use resources locally. My research would gather stories about how people in local neighbourhoods use their abilities, associations, churches, organisations and land to create or solve something.

Luckily we won a big four-year grant that allowed us to go to neighbourhoods all over the United States and Canada, talking to people and collecting their stories. Now I say stories but I never said stories in the university. Stories are worthless at university! There they're case studies. So we collected hundreds of case studies of how local resources are used.

Research is often about discovering patterns in what looks like diverse and disparate information. Ray Mack, the centre director said, "You've got to keep gathering data until it repeats so often that you don't need to go any further."

Any normal, observant person listening to those stories would have begun to notice the patterns, just as we did. And what we saw was that no matter what they were trying to do, there are five resources that people used. They used their individual skills, their associations, their institutions, the land, and their exchanges.

And so as that seemed to us to be really useful information, we then needed to decide on a collective term for the principal resources for getting something done in a neighbourhood.

There was no common term for these five resources so we called them assets. We could have called them resources, or the building blocks of neighbourhoods. But we called them assets.

One of my closest colleagues, Jody Kretzmann joined me in this research. He came from an activist life and he'd been a community organiser too. Throughout all the years developing the ABCD idea, he has remained my constant colleague and close friend. Like me, he came to the university after years of work in Chicago neighbourhoods. Together, we directed the research that resulted in the basic ABCD text – *Building Communities From the Inside Out*. In the subsequent years we both were involved in training thousands of people worldwide while also conducting research resulting in a series of publications that are guides to asset-based development focused on various constituencies. Jody's insights, writing skills and wide-ranging networks have been vital contributions to the growth of the ABCD movement.

Another person who joined us was Stan Hallett.

Stan was a much more theoretical person than I. But he was absolutely applied in his work though he thought conceptually. Stan would say that what happens in many lower income neighbourhoods is that they become dependent on a grants economy.

He coined that phrase, the "grants economy" – if you couldn't get a grant for it, it couldn't be done! Stan said a grants economy plants a concept of money in people's minds, which is that you start out with a lot (of money), and at the end you spend it and have nothing. He observed that most people in the university doing needs research end up with grants.

But Stan said of the research that Jody, I and others were engaged in: "Well, what your research finds doesn't grow out of grants: I haven't heard about grants in any of these neighbourhood stories. So this is the reverse: it's an asset-based economy." Since an asset is the opposite of a grant. It starts small and, if you connect it well, it ends up big. It's a multiplier of what people have, from something little to something bigger, not huge but bigger.

And so that's why we called them assets. They are the local resources that, correctly connected, will create much more together than they do apart.

And it's the connection that is the most important: the asset is always there but the connection and how it's achieved is the critical issue.

So that's how ABCD happened to get named.

CR: You are critiquing the marketplace yet "assets" is pretty much marketplace language.

JMK: Stan Hallett would say that many economists don't think that it is only money that is an asset. There are many economists now who study social capital, which is an economist's definition of social relationships.

CR: And that's the clever thing about the word "asset" – that it challenges people to broaden their understanding of new currencies.

JMK: That's right. Stan Hallett had great influence on me when I was in my forties. He had degrees in divinity and urban planning and was a Methodist pastor in his earlier years. Stan had a powerful intellect. And because he was raised in the rural Dakotas he also had incredible practical skills. He loved to fix things and was an excellent shot. This was because, as a clergyman pastoring several Dakota churches, he was paid a pittance. Therefore, if he was to have dinner, he depended on shooting a pheasant on the prairies as he drove among his small churches.

Stan joined me early in the 70s as we created the Center for Urban Affairs. It was the era when E. F. Schumacher's book, *Small Is Beautiful*, was very influential. It described "appropriate technology" as an alternative to the expensive, polluting, modern machine age.

Stan's thought paralleled that of Schumacher. He created and taught us a powerful abbreviation: FESWAW. It stood for Food, Energy, Soil, Water, Air and Waste.

Stan said these were the six essentials of life, and each was interrelated with all the others. Modern technology constantly broke these relationships, thus degrading the productive use of each essential. So "appropriate" technology was a way to use tools, so they respected and supported the primary life-giving FESWAW relationships.

At our Center, Stan, joined by his student Scott Bernstein, hatched a new organisation and movement. They created the Center for Neighborhood Technology in Chicago, and it continues to be a vital centre of the movement, creating Illich's "tools for conviviality" rather than modern technology that so often creates desolation.

Stan also taught us that there were two kinds of tools. His name for them was a "unitility" and a "multility." His example of a "multility" grew out of our work building a greenhouse on the top of a flat-roofed, two-flat apartment on Chicago's West Side.

On the West Side, thousands of two and three-story buildings had flat roofs. Stan thought this was both wasteful and a great opportunity. He persuaded us to build, on the top of one two-story flat, a simple greenhouse that came from a kit. It was made of plastic panels and a wooden structural framework.

On the roof, we learned that this simple hand-built greenhouse had many "outputs":

> 1. It captured the heat escaping from the roof, using it to warm the greenhouse.
>
> 2. As it captured the heat and held it on the rooftop, the greenhouse reduced the necessity for more heat in the building, thus reducing energy costs.
>
> 3. It captured the sun, thus adding to the seasonal growing capacity.
>
> 4. It produced nourishing food.
>
> 5. It produced income from the sale of surplus food.
>
> 6. Older local residents, often raised in rural areas in the South, began to come to the greenhouse and grow food. This

activity often revived them, physically, mentally and spiritually, enabling more healthful lives.

7. A local school began to bring young students to learn about agriculture and energy conservation.

In these ways, a simple tool made of basic materials produced energy savings, nourishing food, income from sales, and health for seniors and education for students. Stan said it had *low inputs* and *high outputs* – a multility.

Stan's contrast with the greenhouse was an electric toothbrush. It required copper from Montana, steel from Brazil, rubber from Sumatra, oil from Saudi Arabia, costly and polluting systems to get these materials to a place of manufacture, complex machines to process and assemble the materials and hours of labour involved in all elements of the process.

Having created a machine with prodigious inputs, its output was the saved energy for a person who no longer needed to move a brush up and down, back and forth across their teeth. Stan said the electric toothbrush was the perfect modern tool with high inputs and low outputs – a unitility that broke the FESWAW around the world.

It was a great lesson for me. Since then, I have always understood that our work should be post-modern, seeking invention and production that is measured by two standards:

1. Low inputs and high outputs

2. Respect and enhance FESWAW

One other gift from Stan was his telling me that my work had a name. At the time, I didn't know it. Stan said that I was basically involved in promoting the associational world. An association was a small group of citizens whose joint work was a multility – low inputs and high outputs.

Every association is a set of connected people whose collective effort is based on the multiplication of the gifts and capacities of each member. Thus, it is a set of natural relationships where the sum is greater than the parts. It is the social equivalent of appropriate technology.

Then Stan urged me to read the work of Alexis de Tocqueville. Tocqueville's work opened an entirely new understanding of our work. After reading his book, *Democracy in America,* I came to see clearly that relationships of local citizens in associations are the atomic elements of molecular democracy.

Stan passed away during my mid-nineties, but his lessons have been abiding and became central to the conceptualisation and practice of ABCD.

Peter Block, photo public domain

Interview Nine – Peter Block

*There are incredible possibilities if we are willing to
fail to be gods.*

CR: Pulling some of the threads of our conversation so far
together a little, I'm thinking of E.F. Schumacher's wonderful
observation around the great capacity of ordinary people to
take the broad view, and how the great disablement of
professionalism is specialisation. Specialists are compelled to
take the narrow view and are rewarded for it.

You've recently been working with Peter Block, someone who shared that awareness of the limitations of big institutions and another person who has influenced you. Can you talk to me a little bit about that collaboration?

JMK: Peter spent a lot of his life as an organisational consultant with big institutions, governments and agencies, and mostly corporations. When the field started, organisational development was very mechanistic and about managerial control. Peter and a couple of other people were the creators within that field of what I'd call "humanistic organisational development." If you think of an institution as a place made up of people who work in groups, the question might be, "How does this work satisfy you?" as well as satisfying the managers. Peter was a central steward of that question.

Peter has written a lot of books for managerial people and the world he knows is largely unfamiliar to me.

He began to look around for collaborators, to make a learning path that would be useful outside of institutions. We met each other and he asked me to come and do something with him. And so we got to hear each other in more detail. Peter said I should write a book. I told him I'm not a writer, I'm a speaker! And he said, "Well, would you write one with me?" I said I'd be delighted. So that's how we got started on the book that's titled *The Abundant Community*.

So I would periodically go to Cincinnati where Peter lives and we recorded our discussions about community. He typed a transcript of the tapes, then we'd read them through and talk for a day or two more. And from reading the transcripts again there emerged a pattern. He's better at figuring out the pattern than I, so he began to set up a framework. The book is the result of probably 10 or so discussions.

Every time I went there we would define a group of people of a certain type— for example upper-class women, working-class

Germans, African Americans, and people from the hills in Kentucky —and he'd get a group of them together in his living room. Then we'd sit down with these people and talk with them about their idea of community. Those discussions were very instrumental in shaping our community understanding. We (Peter and I) were from very different worlds and yet had many complementary views and visions.

CR: As a chapter in your life, how does this period sit alongside other periods? Aside from the obvious differences in background, is your collaboration with Peter different in any way from other collaborations?

JMK: Yes, we're two old guys and if you learn anything from life this is the time when you know it. You're probably not going to learn much more.

So I think if I'd met him 30 years ago I don't know if we'd have been nearly as compatible because we wouldn't have got to the places we have with our work. We've come together toward the end of our lives in a very synchronous understanding of what makes a good life. For me, Peter added a great emphasis on the personal.

CR: Tell me more about that.

JMK: Well, he thinks intimacy amongst people is essential for useful, positive, productive things to happen. In all the organising and group stuff I had ever done, I would never have used the words "intimacy," or "personal". However, Peter helped me see that the most important community asset, the gifts of individuals, is deeply personal, not just words or categories. Most people are so institutionalised that the personal gifts are submerged below ground. Yet giving these gifts is the most powerful thing they can do in life.

CR: You both have clicked at so many levels, I would say both you and Peter have a deeply personal connection, which comes across in your work together. It's the unspoken gift of that book.

Section Three: Looking Forward

"ABCD and politics of small things"

3.1 The Essence of Asset-Based Community Development "There's No Place Like Home"
by Cormac Russell

> *"Well, I... I think that it... that it wasn't enough to just want to see Uncle Henry and Auntie Em... and it's that if I ever go looking for my heart's desire again, I won't look any further than my own backyard; because if it isn't there, I never really lost it to begin with."*
>
> (Dorothy Gale, Wizard of OZ)

In the *Vanishing Neighbor*, Marc Dunkelman writes about the changes in the social architecture of American neighbourhoods. He notes that adults today relate differently than did their grandparents, tending towards a few intimate relationships (the inner ring) and a wide expanse of more distant surface relationships (the outer ring). The casualties are the relationships in between (the middle ring). These "in-between" relationships are characterized by conviviality, and fellowship without intimacy, what the Ancient Greeks referred to as 'philia', and what we today refer to as civic connections or association. Dunkleman attributes the erosion of the middle-ring to a range of factors including hyper-individualism technology, greater mobility, and the growing disconnect with institutions that once mediated the space between civic life and bureaucratic structures.

> "We've been empowered in nearly every aspect of our lives to move past many of the burdens that once prevented us from pursuing our personal interests and concerns", he writes.

The seemingly endless pursuit of our "true self " has sought to fill the hollowness of the middle ring and in so doing has further eroded our associational life and ecological stewardship. *Nurture Development*, my social enterprise, was established 22 years ago —as a strategic partner with the Asset-Based Community Development Institute—to support citizens and community practitioners to strengthen the "middle ring." Since then our core objective has been to support organisations and communities to redefine what is traditionally meant by the term 'development', and terms like "helping," in practice as well as in theory. To do so we have invited organisational change makers and social explorers to adjust some of their traditional co-ordinates and…

Instead of asking, how they or their organisations can create more value to/for or with communities of place, to ask how they can make more space for communities of place to create what they value?

Simultaneously we have invited communities of place, as an alternative to top-down institutionally led change, to consider…

Instead of asking how outside agencies can create more value to/ for or with us, to ask how we can create what we value first using local assets, and after we have done that, partner with outside agencies to have them appropriately match our local assets?' Thereby ensuring that outside agencies become an extension of community capacities, not a replacement for them.

At the heart of our objective to redefine "development" and "helping approaches" has been the Asset-Based Community Development (ABCD) approach, the heritage of which has been the subject of this book. By now it should be clear to the reader that Asset-Based Community Development is a description (not a model) of how local residents grow collective efficacy [1] and what they use to do so [2]. The work of ABCD involves paying attention to what is in a local place (what are termed assets); not what we think should be there, or what isn't there. It's been a while since we mentioned what these assets include, so here they are again:

- The gifts, skills and passions of local residents
- The power of local social networks/associations
- The resources of public, private and non-profit institutions
- The physical and economic resources of local places
- The stories of our shared lives, heritage and culture.

The practice of identifying, connecting and mobilising these six assets is a messy and complex endeavour that does not come with a map attached. ABCD is however deeply root in five core principles.

The 5 Core Principles of ABCD

The Asset-Based Community Development approach has a set of principles, which act like a compass not a map. The five core principles of ABCD are:

1. Placed-based
2. Citizen-led
3. Relationship-oriented
4. Asset-Based
5. Inclusion-focused

1. Place-based: Small local places are the stage on which a good, sustainable and satisfying life unfolds. Seeing the neighbourhood as the primary unit of change is a powerful strategy for addressing some of our most intractable socio-economic challenges. It is, however, a strategy that is counter-cultural, in that it seems to contradict the vast swathe of helping interventions which tend to see individuals and institutions as the most legitimate domains for change, to the exclusion of communities of place, their economies, cultures and ecologies.

While personal transformation and institutional interventions have their place, we have seen that by intentionally organising relational power at neighbourhood level, local residents, can connect local human, associational, environmental, economic and cultural resources together and by aggregating them at a hyper-local level come up with incredibly inventive solutions which are not within the reach of top-down institutions.

Neighbourhoods, small towns, villages and estates are the scale at which local residents come to believe they can make an impact. This neighbour to neighbour impact is not about service provision, it is about neighbourliness. A small local place also provides the context within which the multiplicity of helping agencies (each currently working within their own silos) can agree on a common ground that automatically takes them beyond their administrative boundaries, to work across silos in service of all residents.

"Neighbourhood" is therefore the context and scale within which potentially everything can come together, where relational and civic power can, when needed, join with enterprising individuals and the power of civic professionals and their institutional resources. In sum, places can exist and thrive without people, but people cannot exist and thrive without places. Therefore, advocating for health, safety, learning, prosperity or justice, while behaving as though they have nothing to do with our places and cultures is like choosing to grow a flower in a potted plant with limited soil, when we have an entire meadow at our disposal.

2. Citizen-led: There are certain things that only citizens, in association with one another and the assets around them, can do. ABCD is focused on this domain of change. From this inside-out, citizen-led perspective, socio-political, cultural, environmental and economic change efforts, are viewed through the lens of the following questions:

> •What is it that residents in communities are best placed to do together?

•What is it that residents can best do, with some outside help?

•What is it that communities need outside agencies to do for them?

The sequence in which the above questions are asked is critical. If you are a helping practitioner using ABCD principles and practices, you would therefore start by inviting local residents to ask of each other: "What can we do best for ourselves and each other here?" (a version of the first of the three questions above). By engaging with that question, people are enabled to identify, connect and mobilise what they have, to make change happen. That puts them in the driving seat of change as the people with the ability to decide what is to be done, how it is to be done, and who is to do it. In this way they take the lead by using what they have, to secure what they need. In this way, residents also assume a powerful lead in directing outside helpers in how they can best be served. Since, until residents know what they have which is local and within their control, they cannot know what they need from outside (what is not local and not within their control).

3. Relationship-oriented: While ABCD considers every person as having irreplaceable gifts, skills and passions, as an approach it goes beyond individuals and their capacities (without supplanting them), to tap into relational power. Sadly, the power of relationships tends to be undervalued in industrialised, individualistic societies. Notwithstanding, relational power (outside of hierarchical structures such as the workplace) presents an incredible, often-untapped force for good, and as such continues to be the primary energy source for social movements throughout the world.

Relational power enables consensual 'grouping-up' or hive like behaviours that amplify and multiply the capacities of individuals, ensuring the associational whole is greater than the sum of its individual parts. This is not to say that the individuality of members does not matter, it does, the key message here is that for us to have a good life there are certain things we need to do with each other as neighbours, that we cannot do alone, such as creating mutuality, cultivating cultural 'ways', stewarding local economies and the land all require relational power. Further to this relational power, also referred to as associational life, as Dr. Robert Mendelsohn taught us, is a key determinant of:

- Individual wellbeing,
- Public safety,
- Response to natural disasters, and
- Vocational opportunities, to name but a few.

4. Asset-Based: The starting point for ABCD is with what's strong, not what's wrong. Some misunderstand this as an attempt to minimise life's challenges, or normalise injustices. Nothing could be further from the truth. ABCD is the process by which relational power is mobilised to produce a sustainable and satisfying life and culture. With that in mind, starting with what's strong enables local people to get organised to address what's wrong and in making what's strong even stronger. It also allows us to ask searching questions of those who seek to define certain neighbourhoods by the sum of their deficits, and in so doing challenge them to open their eyes and to see what is actually before them. Being actively present to the capacities and resources that exist in every community (which include the gifts of individual residents, associational inventiveness, environmental fruitfulness, cultural heritage, and economic possibilities) becomes difficult when you view the people and place you serve by the sum of their problems. To really show up in a neighbourhood you've got to set aside the utopian impulses to fix, save and deliver, and instead be curious, collaborative and humble.

5. Inclusion-focused: Communities have imperceptible boundaries, inside which are those deemed to belong, and outside which are those considered to be strangers. ABCD therefore, as well as supporting residents to discover and connect local assets, is about actively creating a welcome for "strangers" at the edge of those

social, political, economic and cultural boundaries. Since there is nobody whose gifts are not needed, when it comes to creating an environment within which everyone's gift is given and received, inclusion is a foundational principle of all enduring community building.

5 Principles in a nutshell

In short, the five principles of ABCD are about investing in the group life of the neighbourhood, recognising that collective efficacy is measured not by the strengths or capacities of its leaders, but by the power and connectivity of its groups and their connectivity to each other, their ecology, culture, economy and the gifts of those at the edge.

Stories from the field

To bring this point to life allow me to share two examples from our Learning Sites (ABCD demonstration sites) in the United Kingdom. By way of context, Nurture Development have supported the establishment of ABCD demonstration sites throughout the UK. We work with hundreds of neighbourhoods in the UK and indeed throughout the world in 35 different countries. Here are just two stories of thousands.

Lockleaze, Bristol, Southwest England

A resident in Lockleaze had an idea to offer their neighbours the opportunity to affordably eat out together as a family. Sam (a community development worker) connected her with other residents who were interested in cooking and the idea then grew to become a community supper where people would also learn about the culture and background of the different people in their community The first Lockleaze Community Supper was held before Christmas of 2016 at The Cameron Centre and saw 45 people enjoy foods from Portugal and Jamaica, and learn about the cultures of both countries.

Denise and Lakisha who organised the first supper along with Sue are now looking forward to holding more suppers with their neighbours throughout 2017 and working with new people they have met as a result of the first event.

Clayton West, Kirkless, Northern England

Three local residents in Clayton West organised what they called an "Open House" for residents in Clayton West, a village in Kirkless, Northern England (between Manchester and Leeds). More than 120 people came to share their interests and ideas about their village. While there, people enjoyed chatting with their neighbours—most of whom they didn't know before the gathering—over tea and cake. The purpose was simple, it was about coming together and having fun. During the event people shared their skills and ideas for new groups and activities, such as yoga, knitting, singing. This led to an even bigger more ambitious gathering which took place on 19th September 2015, called *Open Village*.

The Open Village event consisted of a day and evening of events and activities hosted and run by individual residents and local groups throughout the village of Clayton West. Open Village continues to be supported by *Made in Clayton West*, which is an open network of local residents. They are connecting people and skills in the village to help make things happen that make Clayton West an even better place to live on a daily basis. Neighbourliness is the new normal.

Conclusion

The modern credo asserts that "without the marketplace there can be no liberation." I would like to conclude this section—with due regard to the above stories and thousands of other ABCD stories like them – by contesting that credo. Instead I wish to reaffirm the words of the legendary civil rights activist Audre Lorde:

"Without community, there can be no liberation'.

In the final analysis, solutions to the erosion of the "middle ring, if they are to be sustainable, sufficient yet satisfying must:

a) Necessarily step lightly on the planet,

b) Include everyone

c) Place liberation above diagnosis

d) Start with what's strong not what's wrong.

Which is to say, as Dorothy from the Wizard of OZ, would have us remember:

"There's no place like home".

References:

[1] Sampson, Robert J, Jeffrey D Morenoff, and Felton Earls. 1999.'Beyond Social Capital: Spatial Dynamics of Collective Efficacy for Children.' American Sociological Review 64: 633 – 660: http://scholar.harvard.edu/files/sampson/files/1999_asr_beyondsc.pdf

[2] 'Community Capacities and Community Necessities' John McKnight, Co-Director, Community Development Institute Northwestern University http://www.abcdinstitute.org/docs/McKnight%20 Speech%207 – 09.pdf

3.2 The Four Essential Elements of an Asset-Based Community Development Process

The primary goal of an Asset-Based Community Development (ABCD) process is to enhance collective citizen visioning and production through a process that combines four essential elements:

1. Resources
2. Methods
3. Functions
4. Evaluation

1 Resources

Given the importance of the goal underpinning Asset-Based Community Development, the first question to consider is what can citizens use to realize this goal? The answer is local resources, by which we mean six assets or resources which are used to enhance local wellbeing in every sense of the term: associational, cultural, environmental etc. These assets are abundant (there is enough/sufficient amount for everyone and when productively shared they do not run out), universally available (every community has them without exception), and extremely useful to communities eager to get things done to enhance community wellbeing. The six assets are:

1 **Contributions of Residents:** The gifts, skills and passions and knowledge of residents, which are contributed towards the collective wellbeing of their community. Gifts are innate; people are born with them. Skills are what people practice, learn and can teach or share with others. While passions are what people care about enough to take action on. We are particularly interested in civic passions. Passions need not necessarily be rooted in either a given person's gift or skill, but simply a deeply held care, concern or interest. When a person contributes a gift, skill, passion

or a combination of all four, to a neighbour they are engaging in a foundational form of citizenship.

2 **Associations** are clubs, groups, and networks of unpaid citizens, who create the vision and implement the actions required to make their vision, visible, and of consequence. They can be formal, like a Chamber of Commerce, or informal, like a book reading club. An association is the collective word for citizen. As a bird is to a flock, citizen is to an association, and it is within this domain that an individual's gifts, skills, passions and knowledge, when joined with their neighbours, can be amplified and multiplied, so that the whole becomes greater than the sum of its parts.

3 **Local Institutions**, whether for profit, non-profit/non-governmental organization (NGOs) or governmental show up in the civic realm in one of two ways. Firstly, the nature of an institution which acts as a resource toward community wellbeing is to be supportive. The goal of such supportive institutions is to enable citizenship and interdependence at the centre of community life. Supportive institutions consider citizens to be the primary inventors of community wellbeing in a democracy, and see their role as cheering on that inventiveness and serving while walking backwards.

Initiatives can precipitate collective vision-making and citizen production. They do so by:

   a. organizing their supports the way people organize their lives: small and local;

   b. by putting institutional assets at the service of community building efforts and investing in community alternatives to their traditional ways of working;

   c. being clear about what they are not going to do to/for/with communities, because to do so would be to take power from the people they serve;

   d. in the case of government institutions, they create a dome of protection against outside forces that could harm community life.

4 **Local Places:** The main stage on which the above three human resources are revealed, connected and brought into productive collective action, is the built and natural environment. Small, local, bounded places, that people relate to as their shared place: neighbourhood, village, town and so on, provide an optimal threshold within which these resources, can

be brought into right relationship with each other to become connected and mobilized. As well as providing an ideal context for gift exchange, hospitality and revealing abundance, local bounded places are replete with all manner of practical resources that are essential to community life. From the air we breathe to the community gardens we tend, to the places we casually bump into our neighbours or gather in deep fellowship, our shared places root our community experiences.

5 **Exchange:** In the non-monetary world, there are three forms of exchange: 1) the exchange of intangibles, 2) the exchange of tangibles, and 3) use of alternative currencies. In the commercial world 4) there is a fourth form of exchange in the shape of money.

Exchanging intangibles: Through the long history of human exchange between kin, clan, and neighbours, exchanges have primarily been about the circulation of gifts. It is said that a gift is not a gift until it is given; it is also true to say it is not a gift until it is received. Hence why abundant communities nurture a culture of giving and receiving, such exchanges tend to be entered into in a relational, rather than a transactional way.

Exchanging tangibles: involves the bartering or swapping of tangible resources, for example a pig for five chickens, or sharing one lawnmower between six households on a street.

Alternative currencies: like the previous two forms of exchange enable local choice and control. During the Great Depression for instance, many small towns created alternative ways of paying their debt by introducing their own local currencies as an alternative to the beleaguered US dollar. A popular modern example of this is Time Banking, where members of a timebank use their time as a form of currency, each hour of contribution is equal to all others regardless of what is contributed. All three types of exchanges occur within and strengthen the commons (shared civic space) in that they increase gift exchange, they deepen associational life, and encourage hospitality.

The final form of exchange is money-based , and while it is an important feature of community life, we consider it to be the least useful of the four exchanges in producing collective wellbeing, because it operates on the basis of scarcity, not abundance. Money is seen as a scarce resource because it is about debt; in effect it is a promissory note or an IOU. It also tends to operate outside the commons (civic realm) in the realm of private property, in that it does not promote gift exchange, associational life, or hospitality in the way the other three forms of exchange do. Money can often undermine them.

That said, money exchanges, when kept local, can play a powerful hand in nurturing community wellbeing, Credit Union schemes, worker-owned cooperatives, and shop local initiatives are all good examples of this. We also know - based on what we've learned from our friend and faculty member Judith Snow and others vulnerable to not having their gifts recognized and received - that when people have income in place of services and programs (e.g. personal budgets) they can use that resource to enable them to become more interdependent at the centre of their communities and have more choice and control over their own lives.

> **6 Stories:** Local culture, or 'the community way' often finds expression within stories of the people and the 'ways' they have learned through time to survive and thrive within their home places. Hence the sixth resource that enables shared visioning and productivity are community stories. We are all creatures of narrative and when we cooperate with our neighbours in creating and exchanging stories of a more compelling future that respects our traditions, we ensure our culture (our way) prevails. Stories further enable us to pass on important life lessons and traditions to the further generations. Stories also act as powerful connection points between older and younger generations within a community. Local stories therefore, are treasure maps that help us discover the hidden bounty that weaves our cultural assets together, like a tapestry: our cuisines, spiritual beliefs, ways of raising our children, local dialects, and arts are the threads that combine to form this community tapestry. Each tapestry is unique and particular to the place that created it, and to that place alone.

And, as strangers become friends it takes the shape of a mosaic reflecting beauty in diversity.

2 Methods

Having addressed the question of what communities use to co-create their own wellbeing the second question we wish to consider here is: "How do communities go about making those resources productive in a communal sense?"

In answer to this question we note that abundant communities use methods that involve identifying and productively connecting unconnected local resources:

1. Starting with what residents can do themselves as an association of citizens, without any outside help.
2. Then looking at what they can do with a little outside help.
3. Finally, once these local assets have been fully connected and mobilized, citizens decide collectively on what they want outside agents to do for them.

The order is critical. When we start with the third, as often is the case in traditional helping endeavours, we preclude citizen power. The methods that are used vary widely but at their heart they are focused on bringing resources that were previously disconnected together, and supporting them to become mobilized through collective citizen action.

There are countless methods by which communities can connect and mobilize their resources. Suffice to say, Asset-Based Community Development approaches are iterative and emergent. While there are no methods that we can prescribe, there are a number of practices that communities around the world have found helpful. These include:

1. **Discover:** Discovering local resident connectors who naturally weave their community together through neighbour to neighbour and associational relationship building. Convening a table of connectors that

represent the diversity of an entire neighbourhood can be a powerful means of building community throughout that neighbourhood.

2. Welcome: Actively welcoming neighbours and those who are those pushed to the margins, through inclusive learning conversations and listening campaigns. Learning conversations and listening campaigns surface what people care about enough act to upon with their neighbours. Some communities find it helpful to have a Community Organizer (called Community Builders/Animators in Europe) to support these processes. It is important to remember that if a paid practitioner is supporting a community that this is a back-seat role. Local citizens must remain in the lead. Community Organizers can be helpful when it comes to figuring out tactics for deep inclusion and addressing issues of conflict and power imbalance alongside a range of other important functions. They can help build the ship, but they must never become the ship's captain.

3. Portray: As people discover what they care about enough to take collective action, creating dynamic portraits of the local resources that they can use, is a helpful way of making assets visible to everyone. No one person can hold a full picture of all the resources that a community has, so creating a shared and evolving portrait (what some call an asset map) is a powerful method of enabling citizens to discover what resources they already have and to figure out how best to connect unconnected resources.

4. Share: Intentionally doing things together, from breaking bread to tending a community garden, brings us into a radical presence with our neighbours. Sometimes we also create 'shareable moments', where we intentionally create the conditions for neighbours to become friends. Such shareable moments can include skills exchanges, seed swaps, repair cafes. They create a community on-ramp for people who may be unsure about how to get into community life. The more these moments enable gift exchange, hospitality and association the more likely they will become part of a community's way.

5. Celebrate: Celebrating neighbourliness and community life, through food, fun, songs and dance is one of the best and most natural ways to honour our past achievements and dream up new community possibilities.

6. Vision: Creating a collective vision that both sets down the priorities and reveals the possibilities for the shared future of a community is a powerful community building method, which ensures that the community own the process and are the primary producers of it and the actions that flow from it. For some practical guidance on how to facilitate such a process visit: A

3 Functions: The Seven Community Functions.

The third question to consider is; having used methods to discover, connect and productively mobilize local resources, "what essential functions are citizens able to collectively perform that create greater community wellbeing?" The use of the six assets and the methods that reveal, connect and mobilize them enables seven irreplaceable community functions to be performed, namely:

1. ENABLING HEALTH

2. ASSURING SECURITY

3. STEWARDING ECOLOGY

4. SHAPING LOCAL ECONOMIES

5. CONTRIBUTING TO LOCAL FOOD PRODUCTION

6. RAISING OUR CHILDREN

7. CO-CREATING CARE

These seven functions are a critical features of all home-based natural communities. They are also common features of social movements across history, in that they are bottom up, disaggregated, hyper-local and citizen-led. Indeed we believe that whenever a community is engaged in all four essential elements of an asset-based community development process they are acting as members of a powerful and democratic social movement.

No matter how hard they try, our very best institutions cannot do many things that only we can do; and what only we can do is vital to a decent, good, democratic life. Traditional approaches to change making tend towards reform of institutions and a focus on an individual's supposed deficits. Underlying that approach is the assumption that the role of communities is defined as what happens after the important work of professionals and institutions has been completed. The ABCD approach inverts that, highlighting that in a vibrant democracy the opposite is true: the role of professionals is defined as what happens after the community functions are performed.

The following is a description of each of the seven foundational democratic community functions:

☑ **First,** our neighbourhoods and other such small hyperlocal places, when transformed into communities are the primary source of our health. How long we live and how often we are sick is determined by our personal behaviours, our social relationships, our physical environment, and our income. As neighbours, we are the people who can change these things. Medical systems and doctors cannot. Therefore, many epidemiologists find that medical care counts for less than 15% of what will allow us to be healthy. Indeed, most informed medical leaders advocate for non-medical community health initiatives because they recognize their medical systems have reached the limits of their health-giving power.

☑ **Second,** whether we are safe and secure in our neighbourhood is largely within our domain. Many studies show that there are two major determinants of our local safety. One is how many neighbours we know by name, and the second is how often we are present and associated in public – outside our houses. Police activity is a secondary protection compared to these two community actions. Therefore, most informed police leaders advocate for block watch and community policing. They know their limits and call to our community development movement.

☑ **Third,** the future of our earth – the environment – is a major local responsibility. The "energy problem" is our local domain because how we transport ourselves, how we heat and light our homes and how much waste we create are major factors in saving our earth. That is why our movement is a major force in calling us and our neighbours to be citizens of the earth and not just consumers of the natural wealth.

☑ **Fourth,** in our villages and neighbourhoods, we have the power to build a resilient economy – less dependent on the mega-systems of finance and production that have proven to be so unreliable. Most enterprise begins locally, in garages, basements, and dining rooms. As neighbours, we have the local power to nurture and support these businesses so that they have a viable market. And we have the local power to capture our own savings, through cooperative groups, credit unions, and land trusts, so that we are not captives of our notoriously large financial institutions. We are also the most reliable sources of jobs, for in many communities word-of-mouth among neighbours is still the most important access to employment. The future of our economic security is now clearly a responsibility, possibility and necessity for local people.

☑ **Fifth,** we are coming to see that a part of our domain is the production of the food we eat. So, we are allied with the local food movement, supporting local producers and markets. In this way, we will be doing our part to solve the energy problem caused by transportation of food from continents away. We will be doing our part to solve our economic problems by circulating our dollars locally. And we will be improving our health by eating food free of poisons and petroleum. Our backyards and community gardens are therefore primary sites for the production of our health and wellbeing, as well as our local economic renewal and environmental sustainability.

☑ **Sixth,** we are local people who must raise our children. We all say that it takes a village to raise a child. And yet, in modernized societies, this is rarely true. Instead, we pay systems to raise our children - teachers, counsellors, coaches, youth workers, nutritionists, doctors, McDonalds, and YouTube. We are often reduced as families to being responsible for paying others to raise our children and transporting them to their paid child raisers. Our villages have often become useless, often being responsible neither for our children nor our neighbours'. As a result, we talk about the local "youth problem" everywhere. There is no "youth problem". There is a village problem where adults have forgone their responsibility and capacity to join their neighbours in sharing their abundant knowledge with our children. And receiving their wisdom in return. This reconnection and exchange is our greatest challenge and our most hopeful possibility.

☑ **Seventh,** we are the site of care locally. Our institutions can only offer service, not care. We cannot purchase care. Care is the freely given commitment from the heart of one to another. As neighbours, we care for each other. We care for our children. We care for our elders. And it is this care that is the basic power of a community of citizens. Care cannot be provided, managed or purchased from systems. Our way is made possible by the power to care. Democracy is the way we care for our freedom and responsibility. So, it is the new connections and relationships we create locally that build community because in joining each other together, we manifest our care for the children, neighbours and the earth.

Health, safety, economy, environment, food, children and care are the seven responsibilities of our neighbourhoods. They are the necessities that only we can fulfil. And when we fail, no institution or government can succeed – because we are the veritable foundation of a productive society.

Fortunately, at the heart of our movement are three universal and abundant powers that enable us to fulfil our community functions. The three basics of our calling are:

1. The giving of gifts – the gifts of the people in our neighbourhood are boundless. Our movement calls forth those gifts so that they can reciprocated.

2. Second, the power of association – in association we join our gifts together and they become amplified, magnified, productive, and celebrated.

3. Third, hospitality – we welcome strangers because we value their gifts and need to share our own. Our doors are open. There are no strangers here. Just friends we have not met.

Ours is the movement of abundance. There is no limit to our gifts, our associations, and our hospitality. When these three powers are combined, what becomes manifest is a culture of community. A culture can be understood as the way people have learned to survive and thrive in a place over time. That 'way' creates a boundary within which the hidden rules that make a community effective and powerful can be cradled and passed onto future generations, much like 'songlines' among indigenous Australians.

Within a culture of collective visioning and production, as well as having a way to be, health producing; safety creating; good stewards of our ecologies and economies, inclusive of food production; nurturing our own and our neighbour's children; and caring for each other without exception, two other (cultural) capacities are evident:

- The capacity to accept and embrace human limitations, death, and suffering. Life is a terminal condition, we exist within limits, hence our lives are bookended by birth and death. Abundant communities' welcome people's limitations (humanity), accept death and ritualize grief. In so doing they make individual and group suffering not only bearable, but often redemptive and in doing so they recapture death from the medical system and return it to its rightful place at the centre of community life.

- Communities make meaning in the face of mystery. Some people take a utopian approach to the mysteries of life. They believe life is a problem to be solved. Yet, by contrast all indigenous cultures have produced ways to live creatively with mystery, and in the face of the unsolvable have created art forms from poetry to dance, all to share what is perceived sensually, but cannot nor should not be explained logically.

4 Evaluation

The fourth question to consider relates to how we evaluate an ABCD process. The authenticity of everything we do in such a process is evaluated against the primary goal: <u>enhance collective citizen visioning and production.</u> In the preceding three elements we have detailed what is used, how it is done and the functions that are enabled, noting that in general communities use six assets to perform seven functions, using methods that support the discovery, connection and mobilizing of these resources. The fourth essential element of an ABCD process considers how communities take stock of their journey together. They do so by evaluating the extent to which they are engaged with the first three essential elements. This process of engagement is not about auditing, it is about learning, and making midcourse corrections that allow us to stay committed to our cultural calling.

Evaluating an ABCD process therefore requires a move away from traditional top down summative and formative evaluation processes that are features of traditional ways of evaluating community initiatives. Instead an ABCD approach moves towards a developmental and emancipatory learning process.

Here are four ABCD evaluation principles. An effective evaluation:

1. It identifies the maximization of gift exchange.
2. It identifies the maximization and deepening of associational life.
3. It attends to the maximization in the number of participating and co-producing residents and the increase in their citizen power. It places a particular emphasis on the inclusion of those who have been marginalized.
4. Sponsors of ABCD processes ensure that associated evaluations actively conform to the preceding three principles.

1 **Principle #1: Identify the maximization of gift exchange.** The more citizens contribute their gifts to the wellbeing of their neighbours and their community, the healthier, safer and more prosperous all will be. Hence evaluating such reciprocal exchanges offers keen insight into the extent to which a given community is getting stronger.

2 **Principle #2: Associations broaden and deepen:** Abundant communities are made up of associations that a) welcome the gifts of all, b) while allowing sufficient space for diverse associational life to form, and c) facilitating an association of associations to seek a shared vision and work together to produce that vision.

Fig. 1.1 below is a chart that presents the diverse categories of associations that we have encountered in community life around the world. Creating a portrait of the community you live or serve in using this framework will help you create a baseline against which you can see the extent to which associational life is deepening and broadening as a result of your community building efforts.

Fig. 1.1

3 **Principle #3: Evaluate strengthening citizenship.** We can evaluate the quickening of community life by regularly asking, 'are we seeing neighbours whose gifts were not previously received, participating and contributing more?' 'Are we seeing collectives of citizens driving change and feeling more powerful?' 'Are associations in the neighbourhood, coming together to talk about what they can do together, that they can't do alone, and then taking productive action?'

4 **Principle #4: Sponsors of ABCD processes affirm the preceding principles** and ensure they are built into all evaluations. If you are a community worker facilitating an ABCD process or a sponsor agreeing to an evaluation process, ensure that the impacts that are being evaluated are what people in the community say they want to learn from and enable them to do that in a way that is fun and useful to them, and creates a compelling community owned story.

Relationships are the primary currency of community work, not data or money. Hence the preferred learning process is one that values what goes on between people, not what goes on within them as disaggregated individuals. It is not therefore about counting numbers of people who show up, but about cheering on the participation and contributions that deepen community life. Most of the things that matter in life are meant to be treasured, not measured. Hence the accent must remain on learning and sharing not on auditing and counting.

5 What Makes ABCD Distinctive

The central question that we address in this paper is: what makes an ABCD process distinctive from other community support approaches? Our answer is: other forms of community work, often possess one or more, but not all four essential elements (as described above). What makes an ABCD process distinctive then, is the combination of:

1. Resources

2. Methods

3. Functions

4. Evaluation

The diagram overleaf illustrates the relationship between the four essential elements of an asset-based community development process, which is neither hierarchical or sequential. In other words, the elements exist in relation to each other simultaneously and dynamically, so you can start with any one or a combination of the four elements, as long as ultimately you engage with all four. Hence it is only when all four elements are a feature of your community building effort, that it can be said to be an Asset-based Community Development process.

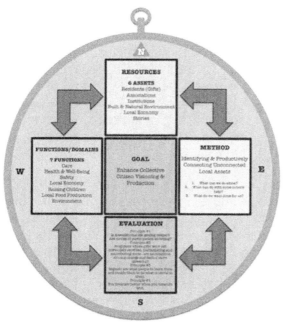

This is not a map, but a compass. Start with any element, but go to element.

3.3 Conclusion by *Cormac Russell*

It has been an immense privilege to sit with John through these conversations that look back into his own journey and that of the Asset Based Community Development story. It is clear to me that John recognises that ABCD simply describes what people do in community life when they are effective. As Alexander Pope put it:

> *"true wit is nature to advantage dressed*
> *what oft was thought*
> *but ne'er so well expressed"*

What John and Jody together have done is to offer a coherent set of observations about effective citizen action within living communities of place, and further to highlight how in modern life such actions are being continually overwhelmed and all too often displaced by consumerism and technocracy. Into the future it is my intention to interview Jody Kretzmann and others who have so greatly shaped the narrative through which we speak about ABCD; this abridged book is the start of that journey.

No one will argue that an extended conversation with John McKnight about his journey and the influences of his fellow travellers, who made the path by walking it together with him, is the most appropriate setting-off point towards a full understanding of the history and heritage of Asset-Based Community Development.

As I reflect on the experience of writing *Looking Back to Look Forward*, my abiding emotion is one of gratitude. I see John's reflections contained herein as among the many great gifts he has brought to the world, and I am grateful to have had the opportunity to spend this time getting to know John in this way.

Too often we think only about the contents of a person's mind, attending solely to their thoughts, and overlooking how they feel and live into what they believe. I take the view that to fully appreciate what John is saying, we need to understand how he makes sense of the world and the practices and principles that help him do so. And so, as we draw to a conclusion on this short book, I'd like to share what I've discovered about the public intellectual and provocateur central to the framing of these ideas: John McKnight himself. Here are my observations.

Firstly, he is an independent thinker. He is a man of unquenchable curiosity, with a sharp and inventive mind. As an independent thinker, he makes sense of the world based on his own observations and experiences rather than just depending on the word of others. While humble, he is completely surefooted around his ability to make judgments, even if (as they often are) they are counter cultural.

As a veteran social explorer he sits easy with the mistakes and dilemmas that inevitably dot the landscape of a life of inquiry, which is as much if not more about the practices that underpin social change, as the thoughts that define it.

Secondly, he is a disciplined thinker, a skilled practitioner in general semantics. The seeming ease with which he take precepts such as: "Words 'don't mean', people do" from general semantics and applies them to reality, is disarming. It flows through him effortlessly, almost as a way of being, ensuring that his default position is to see beyond labels and to resist claims that have no basis in observable reality. His position in near all matters is, "Perhaps this is so. Let's see if it is." As I listen to him, I imagine these well-woven precepts being as much a part of who he is, as the moves of a Tai Chi master. They are imbued within his practice not so much as a discipline but as a way to be in the world.

There is an analogy in general semantics that words and statements are like maps that describe territories. It serves to remind us that words, like maps, only represent reality itself: the map is not the territory. John throughout his long career has remained hugely sensitised to the fact that many people, and even whole institutional systems, live by inaccurate maps; they have incorrect definitions or perceptions of people, places and things. They judge people and events through the labels they assign them, such as "needy," rather than through observable actions and verifiable accounts.

In the preceding pages John emphasises the importance of constructing accurate mental and verbal maps of people, their places, the manner in which they associate, and the institutions that are there to serve them. In general semantics parlance John would be described as "extensionally oriented" in that he is aware that his verbal maps are never identical to the territory they represent.

Thirdly, John is an uncommon, often unorthodox thinker. Illich thought of him as "a natural," and adopted him largely because he came into the world "made this way"; utterly atypical of most thinkers, he has remained unaffected and remarkably open to what may lie over the crest of the next hill. As I interviewed him I could hear this openness in how he answered my questions. It was as if we were unwrapping a present from a dear mutual friend, with all of the expectation and possibility that brings. John demonstrates this openness not just to new ideas, but also to different types of people and ways of knowing, that is utterly uncommon.

I expect this calibre of openness is grounded in large part in the fact that John abjures specialisation. Most academics are the opposite. They spend their careers deep diving into a subject within a discipline, while John continues to spend his life deep diving into life. Because of this he is not taken in by any one approach, way, theory or person. He decides for himself, and digests and tries out and mixes what he learns as he goes. However we may describe this set of traits, it is clear that they set the stage for the kind of multiple, deep influences explored throughout this book, and are foundational to Asset-Based Community Development as we know it today.

His ideas are also uncommon because often at the time of their development or initial expression, they are neither in vogue intellectually, nor popularly received in broader circles. Yet he is not driven by a desire to be different or novel, he does not try to be uncommon in his thinking, he simply is an uncommon thinker. And that is because his ideas are the moral and intellectual essence of who he is, where he comes from, albeit informed and even shaped by whom he admires and wants to engage with.

The people who have most influenced John are not people necessarily known to each other, although they might read and or be aware of one another. Nor, for the most part are they people who ambled into John's life in a pedestrian sort of way. Instead, like kindred spirits, they found John or were linked to him by a connector, and then went on to actively join with him as co-conspirators in a shared inquiry. John is exploring a different way, using a different map, searching for new routes and each of the people that he cites here are companions on that journey, those he counts not as informants or advisors but as friends.

In a world where the map has been pre-agreed, the goals pre-defined, and the worthy end prescribed, John says: "Maybe it is so, let's see; but let's also see what's over there."

Fourthly, he is an applied researcher. His primary concern is what is happening in the field, which is to say communities of place: neighbourhoods, and more particularly at the block level. To this day he is most eager to learn what happens when people become productive together at the neighbourhood scale, since this, he believes, is where our greatest hope for the future lies. He is absolutely convinced of the merits of hyper-localism and what animates him most are conversations that revolve around "local people doing stuff, their way."

Fifthly, John is a classic rhetorician. He is widely recognised as a great orator and an eloquent public speaker, but he is so much more.

Throughout the interview and over the years that I have known him, he has often said that he considers himself more a speaker than a writer. But that has never sat easily with me, since I have seen him use both mediums to great effect and in a very particular way. A rhetorician is practiced in the art of discourse, which in turn seeks to inform, persuade, or motivate particular audiences in specific situations, through the spoken and written word.

For John, learning is a civic practice, primarily grounded in clear observance of the territory, but then thrust out into the commons. This style of communication is a vehicle through which learning deepens but not without some risks. The rhetorician is far from ambivalent about what they want to achieve in communicating with their fellow citizens, they are clear about the stakes and the purpose of their communication. The stakes equal a better democracy. The purpose therefore is to invite others to connect in active citizenship. In practice, to be productive where they live: "Are you a citizen of this place, or do you just live here?"

John would, I think, fare well as an Ancient Greek or classical Roman orator. Indeed, close attention to his writings and speeches reveal the five cannons of rhetoric: invention, arrangement, style, memory, and delivery. That said, he is not a classic scholar. He is a public intellectual and provocateur.

His audience is: Everyman.

It would also be fair to say that John would consider the above description as overly effusive and unwarranted, and that too is the measure of the man.

Foregrounding these five characteristics of John's thinking helps in understanding how the circle of friends that are mentioned throughout this book, have shaped John's thinking and living practice, and adds an essential mixture of light and shade to the themes discussed throughout the text above.

Beyond the above tribute it is profoundly difficult to know how best to conclude what are for the most part John's reflections. Personally I don't believe they are for concluding, they remain ever open and evolving. Perhaps then this is not a conclusion, but rather a holding note in advance of the next chapter. As the Greek Proverb has it:

> **"A society grows great when old men plant trees whose shade they know they shall never sit in."**

I leave you with some of the personal reflections that have stirred up within me, through the course of these interviews:

Perhaps we do not need more start-ups; we need more upstarts, heretics and genuine radicals.

Perhaps seemingly useless small things can be the solutions to our biggest problems.

Perhaps people are not vulnerable in themselves, but how we organise as a society means some people are more vulnerable to oppression and not being able to share and receive gifts than others.

Perhaps children raise parents, and pupils teach teachers, and patients heal doctors and nurses, especially when those children have been nurtured in the community way.

Perhaps the Left thinks the Right is wrong, and the Right thinks the Left is wrong, and that's what's wrong.

Perhaps we are not self-reliant, we are other-reliant.

Perhaps our pursuit of absolutes is serving to create more uncertainty and fragmentation.

Perhaps our need to heal, teach, parent, lead and rescue are as harmful as our more aggressive drives towards having power over others.

Perhaps the enemy at the boardroom table is a friend at the kitchen table.

Perhaps we need fewer leaders who say "this is the way" and more connectors who help us co-create 'our way'.

Perhaps?

Appendix I: 10 Books That Had the Greatest Influence on My Thinking by John McKnight

1. Scott's International Stamp Album

In my youth, collecting used postage stamps opened magical windows into the world. I learned so much about the history, leaders, flora and fauna of almost every country from these little pieces of paper. That knowledge led, early on, to a fascination with all kinds of people and cultures. Later, it led me to be a relentless traveller and an advocate for inclusion.

2. Out of the Night by Jan Valtin

My parents belonged to the Book of the Month Club; in 1941, when I was ten, Valtin's book arrived and I read it. He was a communist who was brutally tortured in an early Gestapo prison. I was horrified by his description and it created a deep youthful commitment to opposing dictatorships, oppression and limits on freedom of speech.

3. Reveille For Radicals by Saul Alinsky

In 1946, when I was 15 I found Saul Alinsky's newly published guide to community organising in our local public library. It was a revelation that you could have a vocation as an organiser. I thought, "That's what I want to do as a living." The fact that Alinsky was based in Chicago was a factor in my deciding to go to Northwestern University. *Reveille* is still the most basic guide book for understanding how people become powerful when they act together. This principle has guided me all the years since I read the book and led me to practice the art of community organising in Chicago neighbourhoods.

4. Deschooling Society by Ivan Illich

In 1969 I met Illich at Chicago's Urban Training Center. I was speaking about five different approaches to school reform. After Illich heard me we had lunch and he asked, most graciously, how I came by the curious notion that schools had something to do with education! This book makes clear why he asked that question. All of his books are among the most mind expanding texts I ever read. He was a lifelong friend who demonstrated to me that life's greatest gift is friendship.

5. De-managing America by Richard Cornuelle

Cornuelle was a Vice-President of the National Association of Manufacturers. One day in the late sixties, he decided to quit his job and take a journey talking with front line industrial workers about what they do. He wanted to understand their work because he had concluded, as an executive, that nothing significant is produced in the "front office" of institutions. The result was this book—a wonderful analysis of how "management" is the problem, not the solution. I met Dick in our later years and we had a brief, but wondrous friendship glorying in the values of associational life.

6. The Making of Blind Men by Robert Scott

Scott, a prominent Princeton sociologist, conducted a major study on the history of service agencies for the blind. This book is based on that study which found that on measures of functionality, blind people who were not served by blind agencies did better than those who were served. To understand how helping can hurt, this book is a landmark study. It demonstrates how service agencies often create dependency and distort the lives of their clients. Unknowingly, they create a culture which makes "blind men." And yet, free of that institutional culture, people who are labelled blind create for themselves a more functional being.

A related very readable study that makes the same essential point about people who don't hear is "Everyone Here Spoke Sign

Language" by Nora Groce.

7. Centuries of Childhood by Phillipe Aries

As *The Making of Blind Men* demonstrates how the blind institutions created "blind men," this book describes how different societies have, throughout time, created "childhood." It helped me see that children, in our time, are social inventions. They behave, believe and act in a world we create for them because of what we uniquely believe a "child" is. This book helped me see clearly that there is no "youth problem." There is a problem with what we believe children "are" and how we create them.

Another book that I found to be an applied use of Aries' insights is, *A Summons to Life*, by Robert Woodson. Woodson writes of his journey to discover effective ways to redefine "deviant childhood." An old friend, Bob, discovered the world outside the culture of youth agencies that create self perpetuating problems called dysfunction, deviance and troubled youth.

8. Last One Over the Wall by Jerome Miller

Scott and Aries demonstrate how we create worlds for vulnerable people in the name of help. Jerry Miller, a wonderful friend and human being, was a professor at Ohio State University who understood that "juvenile delinquents' are an institutional invention. He was hired to "reform" the juvenile justice system in Massachusetts and came to see that reforming the system was impossible. Therefore, he closed all the juvenile reformatories in the state and created opportunities for the inhabitants, their friends and allies to invent new definitions for their lives. This book is Jerry's telling of the most radical institutional "reform" of the twentieth century.

9. No Contest by Alfie Kohn

Kohn, a social psychologist, has written the book that, blessedly, disturbed my students at Northwestern University more than any other. He gathered evidence over many years regarding whether cooperation or competition are more effective methods for achieving our personal and social goals. His startling evidence is that cooperation beats competition most of the time –most clearly as a mode for education. We are so swathed in the culture of competition that it takes a guy like Kohn to lead us outside our competitive consumer world so that we can see that competition is the way to shoot yourself in the foot on your journey towards a good life. He also argues that competition is just a special mode of behaviour developed by patriarchy to keep its dominance.

10. The World I Live In by Helen Keller

Helen Keller was born in 1880 in segregated Tuscumbia, Alabama. Because of a disease at 19 months, she became deaf and blind, cut off from the outside world. Nonetheless she emerged as one of the most influential leaders of the twentieth century. She was an advocate for the rights of women, blind and disabled people, and an active pacifist, socialist, founder of the American Civil Liberties Union and member of the International Workers of the World (Wobblies). President Lyndon Johnson awarded her the Presidential Medal of Freedom, America's highest civilian honour.

Many people asked Keller what it was like to be blind and deaf. How did she become so noteworthy with such physical limits? This book is her answer. I found it a revelation in understanding the source of the power of our personhood. Keller said there are "five-sensed" people and she was "three-sensed." Her story is a glorious paean to our senses—the source of our possibility. The more I read her reflection on the senses, it became clear to me that the institutional, corporate and political systems of our time are basically engaged in an assault on our senses so that we lead senseless lives filled with nonsense. Read this great woman's instruction on how to be sensible—even sensational!

Appendix 2: Publications by John McKnight

2010s

McKnight, J., Block, P., and Brueggemann, W. (2016). An other kingdom: Departing the consumer culture. New Jersey: John Wiley & Sons, Inc. Hopes, K., McKnight, J., and Lawrence, H. (2015, May). Asset based neighborhood organizing: The method of the abundant community initiative in Edmonton, Canada. Evanston, Illinois: Asset Based Community Development Institute.

McKnight, J. (2015, 13 January). Low-income communities are not needy— they have assets. Faith and Leadership.

McKnight, J. (2014, Spring). Building a hopeful future. Connections, 2.

McKnight, J. and Block, P. (2014). The hidden treasures in your neighborhood. In S. Van Gelder (Ed.), Sustainable happiness: Live simply, live well, make a difference (pp. 101-106). Oakland, CA: Yes! Magazine.

McKnight, J. (2014). A children's guide to dismantling our economy. The Abundant Community.

McKnight, J. (2013, Fall). Neighborhood necessities: Seven functions that only effectively organized neighborhoods can provide. National Civic Review, 102(3), 22-24.

McKnight, J. (2013, 1 May). Sensible life ~ A thought. The Abundant Community.

McKnight, J. (2013, 29 March). Defining "community and "neighborhood."

McKnight, J. (2013, 20 February). Modern Mentoring. Abundant Community.

McKnight, J. (2013). The four-legged stool. Washington, D.C.: The Kettering Foundation.

McKnight, J. (2012, December). What it takes to be a citizen in a community. Unpublished essay.

McKnight, J. (2012, October 28). Opening the neighborhood treasure chest. The New Confluence Project.

Kavaloski, V. and Kavaloski, J. (2012, August). Associations: The vital center of democracy. Voice of the River Valley, 12. [Note: Article is about a presentation given by John McKnight.]

McKnight, J. and Block, P. (2011, Winter). The good life? It's close to home: Rebuilding families and neighborhoods around the gifts each of us offers. Yes!, 56, 48-51.

Hurlbert, W. [Interviewer]. (2010, 24 November). Peter Block and John McKnight: The abundant community. Blog Business Success: Blog Talk Radio. Transcription by W. Lambeth.

McKnight, J. and Block, P. (2010, December). Systems and managers: Their growth threatens our welfare. Leadership Excellence, 17.

McKnight, J. & Block, P. (2010, June). Limits of consumption: Satisfaction can't be purchased.Leadership Excellece,18.

McKnight, J. & Block, P. (2010, May). Abundant community: Rediscover your neighborhood gifts.Personal Excellence, 13.

McKnight, J. (2010). Asset mapping in communities. In Morgan, A., Ziglio, E., and Davies, M (Eds.), Health assets in a global context: Theory, methods, action. New York: Springer.

McKnight, J., and Block, P. (2010). The Abundant Community: Awakening the Power of Families and Neighborhoods. San Francisco: Berrett-Koehler Publishers, Inc.

2000s

McKnight, J. (2009, 5 August). What we need is each other: No matter how hard they try, our very best institutions cannot do many things that only we can do. Yes! Magazine.

McKnight, J. (2009, 8 July). Community capacities and community necessities. Opening remarks at the From Clients to Citizens Forum, Coady International Institute, St. Francis Xavier Univeristy, Antigonish, Novia Scotia.

McKnight, J. (2007). The Summit Negotiations: Chicago, August 17, 1966-August 26, 1966. In D. Garrow (Ed.), Martin Luther King, Jr. and the Civil Rights Movement (pp. 111-145). Brooklyn, New York: Carlson Publishing.

McKnight, J. (2005, January). A new approach to building stronger neighborhoods. Unpublished essay.

McKnight, J. (2005). Asset-based community development. The Journal of Community Work and Development, 7, 18-32.

McKnight, J. (2004, November-December). The economy of good works. Mouth Magazine, 15(4), 16-18.

McKnight, J. (2003, Spring). A twenty-first century map for healthy families and communities. Working Strategies: Helping Families Grow Stronger, 6(5), 1-2.

McKnight, J. (2003) Community and its counterfeits. Common Ground, 143, pp. 2, 29.

McKnight, J. (2000). Rationale for a community approach to health improvement. In T. Bruce and S.U. McKane (Eds.), Community-based public health: A partnership model. Washington, DC: American Public Health Association.

1990s

Kinahan, D. (1999, Spring). When the glass is half full. Who Cares? The Toolkit for Social Change, 38-40.

McKnight, J. and Pandak, C.A. (1999, April). New community tools for improving child health: A pediatrician's guide to local associations. Evanston and Oak Brook, IL: Community Access to Child Health, American Academy of Pediatrics, and the Asset-based Community Development Institute.

McKnight, J., Sidford, H., Ivory, G., Rabkin, N. and Pavlick, K. (1999, January). Cultural assets: A roundtable discussion. Business/Arts Quarterly, 3-13.

McKnight, J. (1999). Philanthropy & the church in the city. In J. Cistone & E. Reichard (Eds.), Common ground for the common good: The church in the city regional forum series proceedings (pp. 62-65). Cleveland: The Catholic Diocese of Cleveland.

An interview with John McKnight: The man who is making an old idea new again. (1998, Fall). Common Focus, 2.

McKnight, J. (1998). Hidden treasure. In M. Larned (Ed.), Stone soup for the world: Life changing stories of kindness and courageous acts of service (pp. 15-17). Berkeley, CA: Connari Press.

McKnight, J. (1998). Turning communities around. Canadian Housing, 15(1), 9-12.

French translation. Aider les collectivités à se reprendre en main. Canadian Housing(Habitation Canadienne), 15(1), 13-16.

Barnett, K. (1997, June). The future of community benefit programming: An expanded model for planning and assessing the participation of health care organizations in community health improvement activities. Berkeley: The Public Health Institute and The Western Consortium for Public Health. [Note: John McKnight is listed in acknowledgements.]

McKnight, J. (1997, May/June). John says: That's pity peddling, misery merchandising—using pity to raise money to pay professionals to create clients. Mouth: Voice of the Disability Nation, 10-11.

Project Friendship Society and the College of New Caledonia. (1997). The Prince George connector: A guide to local clubs, interest and support groups. Prince George, British Columbia: College of New Caledonia Press.

McKnight, J. (1996, November-December). Prepare for the coming One. The Other Side, 6-7.

McKnight, J. and Kretzmann, J. (1996, November). Support from governments for community building. Minnesota Cities, 81(11), 8-11.

McKnight, J. (1996, September/October). A revolution of the senses. The Other Side, 22-28.

McKnight, J. (1996, Fall). Counting in those who have been counted out. The Eagle News / Nociero El Aguila, 13.

Kretzman, J. and McKnight, J. (1996, Summer). Artists as assets for community building. Stone Soup, 14(4), 3. Published by the Neighborhood Reinvestment Corporation.

McKnight, J. (1996, April). Mapping community assets. In Community oriented primary care: A vision for health conference transcripts (pp. 75-86). Health Policy Institute at the University of Texas-Houston Health Science Center.

McKnight, J. (1996). A 21st century map for healthy communities and families. A report of the Asset-Based Community Development

Institute and the Institute for Policy Research, Northwestern University. Evanston, IL.

McKnight, J. (1997, March/April). A 21st century map for healthy communities and families. Families in Society: The Journal of Contemporary Human Society 78(2), 117-127.

McKnight, J. (1995, November/December). Why 'servanthood' is bad. The other side, 56-59.

McKnight, J. (1995, September). Is the helping hand really helping? Front & Centre, 3-4.

McKnight, J. (1995, Autumn). Community: Will we know it when we see it? Wingspread Journal, 8-10.

McKnight, J. (1995, January/February). The asset of local community. Rural Health, FYI: The Magazine of the National Rural Health Association, 17(1), 8-10.

Kretzmann, J. & McKnight, J. (1995). Building communities from the inside out. Health & Developmet, 4, 12-18.

McKnight, J. (1995). The careless society: Community and its counterfeits. New York: BasicBooks.

French translation. La société négligent: La société et ses contrefaçons. Geneve: Editions Des Deux Continents.

McKnight, J. (1994, June 21). Stone walls, iron bars: We can't simply lock up poverty and crime.Chicago Tribune.

McKnight, J. (1994, March). Rethinking our national incarceration policy. In National Criminal Justice Commission: Toward a vision for justice [Conference proceedings].

Cayley, D. (1994, 17 January). Community and its counterfeits: An interview with John McKnight. Ideas, 3(10), 1-26.

Reprint: Cayley, D. (2008, March-April). Community and its counterfeits: An interview with John McKnight. Mouth Magazine, 106.

McKnight, J., and Kretzmann, J. (1993). Building communities from the inside out: A path toward finding and mobilizing a community's assets. Evanston, Illinois: Center for Urban Affairs and Policy Research.

Dutch Translation. Wijkontwikkeling op eigen kracht. National Network of Resident's Associations.

Spanish Translation. Construindo comunidades de dentro para fora.

McKnight, J. (1993). In university and community. In Mike Money (Ed.) Health & community: Holism in practice (pp. 123-134). Cambridge, England: Green Books.

McKnight, J. (1993). Service peddlers versus community believers. Health & Development, 3, 3-7.

McKnight, J. (1993). Taking charge of health in a Chicago neighborhood. In Richard Luecke (Ed.), A new dawn in Guatemala: Toward a worldwide health vision (pp. 219-227). Prospect Heights, IL: Waveland Press, Inc.

McKnight, J. (1992, Fall-Winter). Redefining community. Social Policy, 56-61.

Reprint: McKnight, J. (1996, Summer). Redefining community. Kettering Review, 24-30.

Reprint: McKnight, J. (1997). Redefining community. Inclusion News, 16.

McKnight, J. (1992, 17 August). Diagnosis and the health of community. Evanston, Illinois: Center for Urban Affairs and Policy Research at Northwestern University.

McKnight, J. (1992, 6 February). Two tools for well-being: Health systems and communities.Presented at the Conference on Medicine for the 21st Century. Sponsored by the American Medical Association, The Annenberg Center at Eisenhower, the Annenberg Washington Program, the U.S. Environmental Protection agency and the W.K. Kellogg Foundation.

Reprinted: McKnight, J. (1997). Two tools for well-being: Health systems and communities. In Meredith Minkler (Ed.), Community organizing and community building for health (pp. 20-25). New Brunswick: Rutgers University Press.

McKnight, J. (1991, Spring-Summer). Services are bad for people: You're either a citizen or a client. Organizing, 41-44.

McKnight, J. (1990, 8 November). John McKnight Address to The New Haven Foundation.

Raspberry, W. (1990, 3 April). Above all, 'experts' should do no harm. Chicago Tribune. [Article is about John McKnight's approach to community development.]

McKnight, J. (1990). A British Columbian legacy. Evanston, Illinois: Center for Urban Affairs and Policy Research at Northwestern University.

McKnight, J., and Kretzmann, J. P. (1990). Mapping community capacity. Center for Urban Affairs and Policy Research, Northwestern University.

Reprint: McKnight, J. and Kretzmann, J. (1992). Mapping community capacity. New Designs for Youth Development, 10(1), 9-15.

Reprint: McKnight, J., and Kretzmann, J. P. (2012). Mapping Community Capacity. In Meredith Minkler (Ed.), Community Organizing and Community Building for Health and Welfare (pp. 171-186). New Brunswick, New Jersey, and London: Rutgers University Press.

1980s

McKnight, J. (1989, Summer). Do no harm: Policy options that meet human needs. Social Policy, 20(1), 5-15.

Reprint: McKnight, J. (1996, Fall/Winter). Do no harm. The Community Journal: Building a Better Virginia Together, 12-13.

McKnight, J. (1989). Beyond community services. Evanston, Illinois: Center for Urban Affairs and Policy Research at Northwestern University.

McKnight, J. (1989). Organizing the community. In M.H. Linz, P. McAnnally, and C. Wieck (Eds.),Case management: Historic, current & future (pp. 21-30). Cambridge, MA: Brookline Books.

McKnight, J. (1988, Fall). Building healthy communities. National [magazine of the Canadian Mental Health Association], 3-4.

O'Connell, M. (1988, Septiembre). El regalo de la hospidalidad: Cómo abrir las puertas a la vida de communidad para los impedidos. Northwestern University Center for Urban Affairs and Policy Research. [Note: John McKnight is listed as primary investigator on the project.]

McKnight, J. (1988, Spring). Where can health communication be found? The Journal of Applied Communication Research, 16(1), 39-43.

McKnight, J. (1988, Winter). Centerpiece. Urban Affairs News, 8-9.

McKnight, J. (1987). Communities that help people. Proceedings of the Calgary Service Planning for Alberta's Community Rehabilitation Services. The Spokesman, 3-7.

McKnight, J. (1987). Joyful gerrymanders: Redrawing the social policy map. Jubilee, 4(1), 24-28. Social Concerns and the Episcopal Church.

McKnight, J. (1987). The future of low-income neighborhoods and the people who reside there: A capacity strategy for neighborhood development. Evanston: Center for Urban Affairs and Policy Research.

McKnight, J. (1986, June). Things go better with neighbors (Mary O'Connell interviews John McKnight). Salt, 6(6), 4-11. Chicago: Claretian Brothers and Fathers.

McKnight, J. (1986, Spring). Where do they come from? Forum: The Donors Forum of Chicago, 3.

McKnight, J. (1986, February/March). Social services and the poor: Who needs who? Utne Reader, 14, 118-121.

McKnight, J. (1986). De-medicalization and possibilities for health. In P. Ekins (Ed.), The living economy: A new economics in the making (pp. 122-127). London and New York: Routledge and Kegan Paul.

McKnight, J. (n.d.). Demedicalization and the possibilities of health. Evanston, Illinois: Center for Urban Affairs and Policy Research at Northwestern University.

McKnight, J. (1986). Looking at capacity, not deficiency. In M. Lipsitz (Ed.), Revitalizing our cities: New approaches to solving urban problems (pp. 101-106). Washington, D.C: The Fund for an American Renaissance and the National Center for Neighborhood Enterprise.

McKnight, J. (1986). The need for oldness. Center on Aging, 2, 2-5. McGaw Medical Center, Northwestern University.

McKnight, J. (1986). Thinking about crime, sacrifice and community. Augustus: A Journal of Progressive Human Services, IX(8), 10-16.

McKnight, J. (1986). Well-being: The new threshold to the old medicine. Bulletin of Science, Technology & Society, 6, 1-5.

McKnight, J. (1985, November). Regenerating community. Presentation at Empowerment through partnership: A search conference on mental health advocacy. Ottawa, CA.

Reprint: McKnight, J. (1987, Winter). Regenerating community. Social Policy, 54-58.

Reprint: McKnight, J. (1988). Regenerating community. In D. Gold and J. McGill (Eds.), The pursuit of leisure: Enriching lives with people who have a disability (pp. 9-22). Downsview, ON: G. Allan Roeher Institute.

Reprint: McKnight, J. (1989, Fall). Regenerating community. Kettering Review, 40-50.

Reprint: McKnight, J. (1995, Summer). Regenerating community. Social Policy, 41.

Reprint: McKnight, J. (1999). Regenerating community. In Compton, B. and Galaway, B. (Eds.), Social work processes (6th Edition) (pp. 429-436). Washington, D.C.: Brooks/Cole Publishing Company.

Chandler, C. (1985, November). Interview with John McKnight. Chicago Magazine, 203-207.

McKnight, J. (1985, August). Where can health communication be found? In A Summer Conference of Health Communication (pp. 23-28). Center for Urban Affairs and Policy Research, Northwestern University.

McKnight, J. (1985, Summer). A reconsideration of the crisis of the welfare state. Social Policy, 27-30.

McKnight, J. (1985, May/June). Health and empowerment. Canadian Journal of Public Health, 76. 37-42.

McKnight, J. (1985, May/June). Self-help vs. professional help. Epilepsy Newsletter, 3-4.

McKnight, J. (1985, 17 Febrero). Politizar la atención a la salud. El Gallo Illustrado, 2-4.

McKnight, J. (1985, 3 January). Grief processors: Service technology could kill our sense of community. Pacific News Service.

Young, Q. & McKnight, J. (1985, Winter). Crisis in the social welfare state: Sweden at the crossroads: An interview with John McKnight. Health & Medicine: Journal of the Health and Medicine Policy Research Group, 3(1), 8-12.

McKnight, J. (1985). Perspective: Prevention and poverty. Health & Medicine: Journal of The Health and Medicine Policy, 3(2), 38-39.

McKnight, J. (1985). Health and empowerment. Radical Community Medicine, 22, 34-37.

McKnight, J. (1984, October). John Deere and the bereavement counselor. Foote School, New Haven, CT. Reprint: McKnight, J. (1985, June). Disabling professionals: John Deere and the bereavement counselor. Coping: The Magazine of the Maine Association of Handicapped Persons, 4-5. Reprint: McKnight, J. (1985, September/October). John Deere and the bereavement counselor: Turning community into desert. RAIN, XI(6), 6-11. Reprint: McKnight, J. (1997). John Deere and the bereavement counselor. In Hildegarde Hannum (Ed.), People, land and community (pp. 168-177). New Haven: Yale University Press.

McKnight, J. (1984, 3 Junio). Una reconsideración del Estado benefactor. El Gallo Ilustrado, 5-7.

McKnight, J. and Kretzman, J. (1984, Winter). Community organizing in the 1980s: Toward a post-Alinsky agenda. Social Policy, 15-17. Reprint: McKnight, J. and Kretzmann, J. (1986, Summer). Community organizing in the 1980s: Toward a post-Alinsky agenda. Partner, 1-3.

McKnight, J. (1984). Optimum tools for community health. Bulletin of Science, Technology and Society, 4, 340-344.

McKnight, J. (1983, January/February). The other America. Resurgence, 96, 14-16.

McKnight, J. (1982, Summer/Fall). Impoverishment. Health & Medicine: Journal of the Health and Medicine Policy Research Group, 1(3), 3, 27.

McKnight, J. (1982, November/December). University & community. Resurgence, 95, 10-13.

McKnight, J. (1982, May/June). The two views. Resurgence, 16-17.

McKnight, J. (1982). Health in the post medical era. Health & Medicine: Journal of the Health and Medicine Policy Research Group, 1(1), 2-3, 24.

McKnight, J. (1982). Survival of the family. IETC: Investigative Newsletter on Institutions/Alternatives, 5(4), 1-4.

McKnight, J. (1981, 17 September). Testimony of John McKnight before the Senate Subcommittee on Aging, Family and Human

Services.

Bradford, C. Finney, L., Hallett, S., & McKnight, J. (1981). Structural disinvestment: A problem in search of a policy. In R. E. Friedman and W. Schweke (Eds.), Expanding the opportunity to produce: Revitalizing the American economy through new enterprise development (pp. 125-146). Washington, D.C.: The Corporation for Enterprise Development.

Mcknight, J. (1981). Introduction and prospectus. The University Consortium for Neighborhood Research and Development (pp. 1-10). The Center for Urban Affairs and Policy Research, Northwestern University.

McKnight, J. (1981). Prologue. In R. Hanson & J. McNamara (Eds.), Partners: Neighborhood revitalization through partnership and Whittier neighborhood: A Minneapolis case study.Minneapolis: Dayton Hudson Foundation.

McKnight, J. (1981). Public health policy and the modernized poor. Evanston, Illinois: Center for Urban Affairs and Policy Research at Northwestern University.

McKnight, J. (1980, Fall). A nation of clients? Public Welfare: Journal of the Public Welfare Association, 15-20.

Reprint: McKnight, J. (1986, September). A nation of clients. The Minneapolis Catholic Worker, p. 5-6.

McKnight, J. (1980, Autumn). The future of cities in an urban service economy. The Journal of Intergroup Relations, VIII(3), 25-30.

McKnight, J. (1980, June). The economy of work: Race, cities, and services. Chicago Urban League Research Notes, 17-19.

McKnight, J. (1980, July/August). Community health in a Chicago slum. Health Policy Advisory Center Bulletin, 13-18.

McKnight, J. (1983). Community health in a Chicago slum. Development: Journal of the Society for International Development, 72.

Reprint: McKnight, J. (2000). Saúde comunitária numa favela de Chicago. In Saúde e educação (Health and education) (pp. 105-115). Rio De Janeiro: DP & A Editora.

McKnight, J. (1980, March/April). The professional problem. Resurgence, 79, 16-17.

Reprint: McKnight, J. (1981). The professional problem. The Grantsmanship Center News, 9(1),36-43.

Reprint: McKnight, J. (1981, Winter). The professional problem. The Learning Connection, 2(1), 2.

McKnight, J. (1980). Neighborhood organization, community development, and the assumption of scarcity: The problem of equity and justice. In P. Dubeck and Z. L. Miller (Eds.), Urban professionals and the future of the metropolis (pp. 32-37). New York and London: Kennikat Press.

1970s

McKnight, J. (1979, November). Are we really interested in health or is medical care more important? Paper presented at Community Health Promotion and the Hospital, Bronx, NY.

McKnight, J. (1979, Summer). Old isn't a problem. The CoEvolution Quarterly, 22, 138.

Reprint: McKnight, J. (1980, May). Old isn't a problem. The Witness, 63(5), 7.

McKnight, J. (1979, July/August). The need for oldness. Resurgence, 75, 14-16.

Reprint: McKnight, J. (1979, August). The need for oldness. Ontario Association of Homes for the Aged Quarterly, 15(3), 13-17. (1979, April). Strengthening families through informal support systems. Presented at the Wingspread Conference in Racine, Wisconsin.

McKnight, J. (1978, November/December). Medical colonialism. Resurgence, 12-13.

McKnight, J. (1978, November/December). Organizing for community health in Chicago. Science for the People, 27-30.

McKnight, J. (1978, November/December). Politicizing health care. Social Policy, 36-39.

Reprint: McKnight, J. (1981). Politicizing health care. In P. Conrad and R. Kern (Eds.), The sociology of health and illness: Critical perspectives (pp. 557-563). New York: St. Martin's Press.

McKnight, J. (1978, July/August). The politics of medicine. The New Ecologist: Journal of the Post-Industrial age, 4, 112-114.

McKnight, J. (1978, May/June). Prof. says we need the needy. Northwestern Memo, 15. [reprinted article from The New York Times.]

McKnight, J. (1978, Spring). Good works and good work. The Journal of Portfolio Management, 9-11.

McKnight, J. (1978, January.). The medicalization of politics. The New Physician, 39-40.

McKnight, J. (1978). A cancerous health development: The case of American medicine.Development Dialogue, 1, 14-18.

Center for Urban Affairs and Policy Research at Northwestern University. (1978). Selected letters in response to advertisements requesting information about non-medical approaches to coping with epilepsy. [Collaboration between Steve Whitman and John McKnight.]

McKnight, J. (1977, November/December). The professional service business. Social Policy, 110-116.

McKnight, J. (1977, 16 November). [Op-Ed Page]. Good work, good works. The New York Times. Retrieved from http://www.nytimes.com/1977/11/16/archives/good-work-good-works.html?_r=0.

McKnight, J. (1977, November). Valuable deficiencies. Futures Conditional, 5(3), 16-17.

Reprint: McKnight, J. (1977, Fall). Valuable deficiencies: A service economy needs people in need. The CoEvolution Quarterly, 36-38.

Reprint: McKnight, J. (2001). Valuable deficiencies. Alternatives, 40.

McKnight, J. (1977, 22 May). On the backwardness of prophets. Presented at the Alice Millar Chapel.

McKnight, J., Caplan, J., Illich, I., Shaiken, H., & Zola, I. K., (1977, Reprinted in 1992). Disabling professions. New York and London: Marion Boyars Publishers.

Dutch translation. (1978). De deskundige: vriend of vijand (Disabled Professions). Netherlands: Het Wereldvenster Baarn.

Italian translation. (1978). Le Professioni Mutilanti. (Disabled Professions). Assisi: Cittadella Editrice

Japanese translation. (1978). Disabled Professions. Japan: Shinhyôron.

McKnight, J. (1977, Avril). Le professionalisme dans les services: un secours abrutissant.Sociologie et societies, 9(1), 7-19.

McKnight, J. (1977). On the imperial possibilities of modernized medicine. Evanston, Illinois: Center for Urban Affairs and Policy Research at Northwestern University.

McKnight, J. (1976, 8 October). Professionalized service and disabling help. Paper presented at the First annual Symposium on Bioethics of the Clinical Research Institute of Montreal.

Reprint: McKnight, J. (2000). Professionalized services: Disabling help for communities and citizens. In Don E. Eberly (Ed.), The essential civil society reader (pp. 183-194). Lanham, MD: Rowan and Littlefield Publishers, Inc. McKnight, J. (1975, 16 May). Hospitals must work to change image/ data on public needed.Hospitals: Journal of the American Hospital Association, 40(10), 72-74.

McKnight, J., Bush, M., Dewar, T., Fegan, K., Gelberd, L., Gordon, A., & McCareins. (1975). Al di là del bisogno: La società è servita. In F. Basaglia and F. Basaglia Ongaro (Eds.), Crimini di pace: Ricerche sugli intellettuali e sui tecnici come addetti all oppressione (pp. 471-478). Torino: Nuovo Politecnico.

McKnight, J. (1975). Patient-Sein: ein neues soziales Leitbild? In R. Brun (Ed.), Medizin statt Gesundheit? (Medicine Instead of Health?) (pp. 121-126). Zurich: Gottlieb Duttweiler-Institut.

Illinois State Advisory Committee to the United States Commission on Civil Rights. (1974, May). Bilingual/Bicultural education: A privilege or a right? [John McKnight was the Chairman of the committee.]

Gordon, G., Bush, M., McKnight, J., Gelberd, L., Dewar, T., Fagan, K., McCareins, A. (1974). Beyond need: Toward a serviced society. Evanston, Illinois: Center for Urban Affairs and Policy Research at Northwestern University.

Center for Urban Affairs. (1974). An analysis of the state role in urban educational systems: The case of Illinois. A report to the Superintendent of Public Instruction. Northwestern University.

Illich, I., McKnight, J., & Mendelsohn, R. (1973, June). National health insurance and the people's health. The Cresset, 24-26.

Reprint: Mendelsohn, R., McKnight, J., & Illich, I. (1973, June). National health insurance and the people's health. Clinical Pediatrics, 12(6), 324-325. Reprint: McKnight, J., Illich, I., & Mendelsohn, R. (1973). National health insurance and the people's health. Alternative: Health care, 1-4. CIDOC (Centro Intercultural de Documentacion).

Reprint: Mendlesohn, R., McKnight, J., & Illich, I. (1978). National health insurance and the people's health. In R. Aaseng (Ed.), Viewpoints: Christian perspectives on social concerns (pp. 13-14). Minneapolis: Augsburg Publishing House.

Berger, C., McKnight, J., & Cohen, M. (1973). Attitudes of Chicago suburban influential toward the prospect of low and moderate income housing in their communities. A report by the Center for Urban Affairs at Northwestern University. Evanston, IL.

Downs, A. (1970, January). Racism in America and how to combat it. United States Commission on Civil Rights. Washington, DC. [Note: John McKnight contributed, although not officially listed as author.]

1960s

McKnight, J. (1969, February). Toward a model of relevant inclusion: Indianapolis workshop: A progress report, 65- 72.

McKnight, J. (1968). Community action. In E. Ginzberg (Ed.), Business leadership and the Negro crisis (pp. 161-168). New York: McGraw-Hill.

McKnight, J. (1968). Housing programs and discrimination. In S. Tax (Ed.), The people vs. the system: A dialogue in urban conflict (pp. 229-233). Chicago: Acme Press.

The United States Commission on Civil Rights. (1967). A time to listen...A Time to act.Washington, DC. [Note: John McKnight chaired the Illinois advisory committee to this Commission.]

McKnight, J. (1962). Civil rights and liberties. In The events and personalities of 1961 (pp. 212-214). New York: Spencer Press.

1950s

McKnight, J. (1959, April). The continuing crucifixion. Advance magazine, 1-5.

Undated publications

Berk, R., Mack, R. & McKnight, J. (n.d.). Race and class differences in per pupil staffing expenditures in Chicago elementary schools, 1969-1970. A report by the Center for Urban Affairs at Northwestern University. Evanston, IL.

Bradford, C., Finney, L., Hallett, S., & McKnight, J. (n.d). Community development policy paper: Structural disinvestment: A problem in search of a policy. Center for Urban Affairs, Northwestern University.

Kretzmann, J., McKnight, J. & Turner, N. (n.d.). Voluntary associations in low-income neighborhoods: An unexplored community resource: A case study of Chicago's Grand Boulevard neighborhood. A report of the Asset-Based Community Development Institute and the Institute for Policy Research, Northwestern University. Evanston, IL.

McKnight, J. (n.d.). The service economy. Presentation to the Chicago Urban Leage. [Note: speech likely made in the 1970s or 1980s.]

McKnight, J. (n.d.). Creating a need for daycare. The Doctor's People Newsletter, 2(1), 7-8.

McKnight, J. (n.d.). Communities as problem-solving places. Presentation to the Minnesota Developmental Disabilities Council.

McKnight, J. (n.d.) Elderly need servants, not services. The Doctor's People Newsletter, 2(4), 5-7.

McKnight, J. (n.d.). Homelessness: Growth industry of the 1990s. The Doctor's People Newsletter, 2(4), 2-4.

McKnight, J. (n.d.). Inventing a new America. [Unpublished essay].

McKnight, J. (n.d.). On the productive functions of associations. [Unpublished essay].

McKnight, J. (n.d.). Recommended field study reading list. [Note: suggested reading list given to students at the end of a seminar.]

McKnight, J. (n.d.). The future of low-income neighborhoods and the people who reside there: A capacity-oriented strategy for neighborhood development. Evanston, Illinois: Center for Urban Affairs and Policy Research at Northwestern University.

Gordon, A., Bush, M., McKnight, J., Gelbard, L., Dewar, T., Fagan, K., & McCareins, A. Big brother in a box. The New Ecologist: Journal

of the Post-Industrial age, 5, 158-160.
ABCD Workbooks—supervised by John McKnight and Jody Kretzmann:
McKnight, J. (n.d.). A basic guide to ABCD community organizing. Evanston, Illinois: Asset Based Community Development Institute.
Chicago Law Enforcement Study Group
[Note: The following research reports, supervised by John McKnight, were conducted by the Chicago Law Enforcement Study Group and published by the Center for Urban Affairs and Policy Research at Northwestern University.]
Knoohuizen, R. & Zenner, S. (1975). Discretion and juvenile justice. Evanston, Illinois: Center for Urban Affairs and Policy Research at Northwestern University.
Knoohuizen, R. (1974). Women in police work in Chicago. Evanston, Illinois: Center for Urban Affairs and Policy Research at Northwestern University.
Knoohuizen, R. (1974). The question of police discipline in Chicago: An analysis of the proposed office of professional standards. Evanston, Illinois: Center for Urban Affairs and Policy Research at Northwestern University.
Knoohuizen, R. (1974). Public access to police information. Evanston, Illinois: Center for Urban Affairs and Policy Research at Northwestern University.
Knoohuizen, R. (1973). The Chicago Police Board. Evanston, Illinois: Center for Urban Affairs and Policy Research at Northwestern University.
Knoohuizen, R. (1973). The selection and hiring of Chicago policemen. Evanston, Illinois: Center for Urban Affairs and Policy Research at Northwestern University.
Palmer, D., Knoohuizen, R. & Gordon, A. (1972). The police and their use of fatal force in Chicago.Evanston, Illinois: Center for Urban Affairs and Policy Research at Northwestern University.
Fahey, R. & Palmer, D. (1971). An inquest on the Cook County Coroner. Evanston, Illinois: Center for Urban Affairs and Policy Research at Northwestern University.

Knoohuizen, R., Meites, T., Palmer, D. (1972). Legal materials on police misconduct and civil damage actions in the federal courts. Evanston, Illinois: Center for Urban Affairs and Policy Research at Northwestern University.

Caulfield, B. (1972). The Chicago Police Department: Access to information, personnel practices and internal control–A review of major reports. Evanston, Illinois: Center for Urban Affairs and Policy Research at Northwestern University.

Mercer, S. & Fahey, R. (1971). Trial of juveniles as adults under the Illinois Criminal Code. Evanston, Illinois: Center for Urban Affairs and Policy Research at Northwestern University.

Mercer, S. Gordon, A. & Fahey, R. (1971). Release on bond and legal representatives of criminal defendants arrested in Evanston, Illinois during 1970. Evanston, Illinois: Center for Urban Affairs and Policy Research at Northwestern University.

Lassar, S. (1971). The administration of law enforcement assistance administration grants in Illinois, 1960-70. Evanston, Illinois: Center for Urban Affairs and Policy Research at Northwestern University.

"This wonderful little book represents several profoundly important links in a chain of generous receptivity to the gifts and wisdom of others: to Cormac Russell from John McKnight, to John from some of his most significant teachers, and to each of us, through these carefully attentive friends, from the neighbours in our own places, in the neighbourhoods immediately around us. 'Words don't mean, people do,' says John McKnight. Here is a glimpse of some people who, through their words, invite us to rediscover the deep meanings embodied in friendship, conviviality, and community."

Revd Dr Al Barrett
Rector, Hodge Hill Church (Birmingham, England)

"What a gift this short book is to all of us who yearn and work for 'beloved community.' Cormac's unobtrusive conversations with John McKnight, share kindred creative spirits who helped John's evolution of thought and practice. Through this lens we see the possibility of local citizens sharing their gifts to weave beloved community. We need this look to MOVE forward in these turbulent times."

Mary Nelson PhD, Senior Faculty member of the ABCD Institute, formerly founding President and CEO of Bethel New Life (Chicago, USA)

"Some of the best tools to guide our way into the future may indeed come from the stories of the past. I feel so relieved that this series of interviews captures the experiences and learnings of the man who, so many years ago, utterly transformed my concept of community, and, in turn, the life of my now adult daughter who lives with multiple disabilities. I am now assured that the foundation of the ABCD movement is well documented and secure – a legacy for all future generations. Thank you, Cormac Russell. And thank you, John McKnight!"

Linda Doran Viscardis, CEO of Viscardis & Associates, Passionate
parent
advocate for interdependence in community life, for all.
(Peterborough Ontario Canada)

"Cormac and John have given us all a gift in this book; it's value will truly be seen in the next decades. The subtitle of the book speaks to the place of ABCD in the world today, I cannot speak of the world but I can of its place in municipal life, and I see a skyrocketing demand for the principals of ABCD to be woven into the fabric of every city neighbourhood. These principles are the framework by which neighbourhoods and blocks are becoming strong, caring and supportive social units. This concise and readable book of stories will serve well as a foundational document to support this movements flourishing into the future."

Howard Lawrence
Abundant Community Edmonton (Canada)

"In this age of white noise and zero-sum politics, this collection of McKnight's insights, those who have influenced him and the formation of ABCD is essential reading to center your head and your soul. For any of us seeking to empower community volunteers to build and sustain great places to live, these stories and their wisdom will help all of us, together, find our way forward."

Jeffrey G Yost
Nebraska Community Foundation
President and CEO (USA)

"The reflections about what constitutes a society and how community members may change it, is not only food for thought, but also inspiration to act. The interviews show how Asset-Based Community Development was born from critical thinking, humbleness, and respect for citizens and local cultures, to empower local communities and make changes that matters both locally and globally."

Prof. Rita Agdal,
Head of the community work section, Western Norway University of Applied Sciences (Norway)

"Looking Back to Look Forward is conceived and crafted with belief, hope and inspiration; a summons to pursue alternatives to the abyss of the 'earn-consume' cycle—to go beyond the reform of traditional institutions.

Cormac's gift and ability to carve sentences and passages out of the most relevant and fitting words was so inviting and revealing. I felt as if I were sitting in on the conversations with John McKnight quenching my thirst to pursue my quest towards community-building.

Cormac was able to brilliantly distil decades of evolution of ABCD, expanding the horizon of the reader as every page is sipped with eagerness and anticipation.

Many thanks Cormac for helping me to anchor my commitment and for giving me more possibilities to contribute to the community."

Joseph Maalouf, Member of Parliament (Lebanon)

"This is such an important book, both for newcomers to ABCD and for experienced practitioners of the approach.

It weaves the foundational influences of ABCD, delightfully articulated by John McKnight as though the reader were at a fireside chat, into a wonderful tapestry of core principles for helping every individual, no matter how marginalized, to see themselves, and to see others, as active citizens with important gifts to contribute to the development of their communities."

Gord Cunningham, Assistant Director Coady International Institute, St.
Francis Xavier University, Antigonish, Nova Scotia (Canada)

"Expressed in his own voice, this collection of stories about thought leaders who influenced John McKnight emphasizes John's legendary importance in defining the message that (re)building of communities will not be done by institutions or the experts they hire. Rather, the power to build strong communities anywhere lies in the talents of individuals in neighborhoods and in the strength of the relations and associational life they create. By authoring this book, Cormac Russell has given us all a gift that will keep giving."

Howard Rosing
Executive Director, Steans Center at DePaul University

"For those of us committed to Asset-Based Community Development (ABCD), this book is essential reading. Firstly, it captures the inspiration and insights of John McKnight from whom many of us first learnt and valued the ABCD philosophy and practice. Secondly, it is written by Cormac Russell; no one on the globe demystifies that philosophy and practice better! Wow! What a resource gem as we seek to move the mindset from deficiencies to assets, from clients and consumers to citizens and producers."

Peter Kenyon, Founding Director of Bank of I.D.E.A.S (Australia)

Printed in Great Britain
by Amazon

87274191R00088